# They Said IT Couldn't Be Done But GOD

By

## Virginia Coleman Lee

*So You Can Write Publications, LLC*
*PO Box 80736*
*Milwaukee, WI 53208*
*www.sycwp.com*

*Publishing date: 4/15/2025*
*ISBN-13: 979-8-9899762-4-9*

*Cover design by: www.sycwp.com*
*Printed in the United States of America*

*(Note: "The majority of quotations gathered by the author have been frequently in print and/or movie and television, as well as publicly accessible on the Internet; considered public domain. Where possible, the author and publisher have made their best efforts to credit any available sources for them. In the cases where it was uncertain where they first appeared, the information was cited as "unknown" or "anonymous." The information in this book is intended to uplift and inspire all who read it, or who have it read to them. The information quoted was kept as it was found and/or heard by the author, who makes no guarantee that the information one-hundred percent accurate, just that the author intended for it to be beneficial to all who reads it, or has it read to them."*

SO YOU CAN WRITE
PUBLICATIONS®

# Tables of Contents

Table of Contents

# Dedication

---

This book is dedicated to my husband, Lawrence Lee, not only was he the reason for me writing this book and for always keeping all of your promises and blessing me with a home.

# Prologue

---

Thus, February 1, 2003 my husband and I are celebrating our 34th wedding anniversary today. I have a new look on life and decided to write this journey down on paper because I could not believe that it had been done. But God stepped in.

I have been through too much these past 34 years and even throughout my life. God has provided what I needed at the time. I thank the Lord for blessing me with my parents, grandparents, teachers, church families, communities and the individuals I have worked for down through the years being a maid. He has blessed us to raise our children; they are grown. He has carried us through the storms, thorns and thistles of all our problems.

I give God all the praise because he taught me through his word that he is all I need and I can't change anybody or anything, but give it all to him. This is my prayer… "Heavenly Father, Son and Holy Spirit give me the mind to keep praying and not just in asking but also in thanking you for all things. I thank you for my husband, my children, my home, jobs, health and strength."

This is the beginning of this journey that God started me on. On this journey he has let me know that he would never leave me or forsake me and that he would provide me with all my needs according to his riches and glory, through people that I would have never thought possible. But God!

# Chapter 1

---

## ~*Birth*~

I was born to Emma Mae Simpson Coleman and Eddie Coleman, in Forest Home, Alabama on June 25, 1945. I was born premature at seven months. I was born in my grandparents' home with a midwife. It was said that I was not going to live because I was so small. My grandmother fed me with what she called a 'sugar tit.' She placed a clean white cloth in milk and put it in my mouth for me to suck on. I couldn't nurse on a bottle or from my mom's breasts because I wasn't strong enough. They said it could not be done. But God!

My grandparents were Annie Bell Lewis Simpson and Jim Simpson. They had eleven children, six boys and five girls but they made room for mom and me. My mom was the third oldest. Papa and Mama were married 63-years before she died in 1979, and Papa died in 1982. I called my grandparents Papa and Mama; we all did. I called my parents by their name, Emma and Eddie.

After my mom and I came home from Louisville, Kentucky, that's where we were staying when my parents separated, we lived with my mom's parents. We lived on a hill in a big rented house that Papa rented for $100 dollars a year. Only six of Papa and Mama children were out of the house, four boys were still living at home. Emma cooked, washed and ironed. Mama was able to help for years until her health worsened.

I was the oldest granddaughter. There were two grandsons older and one eleven months younger. One was the oldest girl's son. She was married and her son stayed with her but the other two stayed with us at Mama and Papa's house. Mama spoiled me because I was the only girl. And because she nursed me when I was a baby. She held me day and night to keep warm. Mama took me with her when she went to do work for other people. She did missionary work for the sick and elderly people in the neighborhood. She washed clothes, cleaned and cooked. Jesus was getting me ready.

When we first came home everyone would say that I talked properly. I thought squirrels were cats and when my uncles went hunting I told Mama that they killed all the cats (smile). I remember a little about Louisville. We stayed in an apartment and my mom loved to listen to soap operas on the radio. She would listen to Stella Dallas and Mary Knowber.

One day she was listening to soap operas and the two boys from next door came over and asked if I could go to the fish market with them across the street. They were older so she said yes. They ran across the street not holding my hand so I ran after them. On my way across the street a bus was coming. The driver said he saw people yelling, "Stop! Stop!" So, the driver hit the brakes and came to a complete stop. When he stopped the bus rocked forward and knocked me down and skinned my knees. The police officer took me home.

My mom said she looked up from the radio and wondered why the traffic was held up then the policeman knocked on the door and told her what happened. My mom called my daddy and they took me to the doctor. The doctor treated me. I had no broken bones. The city paid the doctor bill and gave my parents some money. My parents did not sue the city and they requested that the bus driver keep his job. But God! To this day I am fearful of crossing streets, walking in parking lots and of driving.

My dad was from Selma, Alabama so I was told. He was a truck driver for a logging company that moves from place to place. The company moved to Old Texas, a small community south of Forest Home. He married my mom then because she was with him, as well as her brother in law and cousins. They used to sit around and tell jokes. One I remember really well was my grandmother's brother was down there too. We called him Uncle Bubba. He had made him a little bed on the side of the wall and he called it S.O.B, all the other men had to sleep on pallets.

They would try to steal his S.O.B., so he would tell them I am going to knock that S.O.B. down. The other men who were with them were my grandmother's cousins from our small community and another man that wasn't related. These people told me a lot about my dad and also my mother's brother Lee Earnest. Everyone also said, I looked like him until I got older.

Oh! My daddy got in the military because his boss got mad at him and told him if he didn't work for him he would sign him up to go to the army. He meant it for harm but God meant it for good. You know they could do that back then.

God had a plan to make a way for my grandparents, my mom and me.

My dad sent me big boxes of clothes, paper, pencils, pens, tablets, rulers and everything I would need for school. I would take the paper, pencils, pen and crayons to school every day and give it to the children who didn't have any. Another thing my daddy sent me was a purple shirt with three lambs on the front. The center one was down and the other two were up higher. It was my favorite shirt and when I couldn't wear it anymore Mama put it in a quilt. I don't know what happened to that quilt.

My dad helped in more ways than I realized. When I was older one of the children that I shared paper with back then used to tell me every day that she left hers at home. I believed her. After we were grown she came to me and said she didn't forget the paper but she didn't have any at home. She told me, "You never said no!" My daddy helped again. But God.

I always wanted my daddy in my life especially when I thought my mom and grandparents were being mean and not letting me have my way. I started writing this book and remembered all the ways he had touched my life. Not there? But he was there. Thank God.

My dad also gave me a low, cowhide bottom chair. It was just my size. I would rock in the chair as if it were a rocking chair until one day Papa told me to stop but I didn't. I rocked so high until the chair fell backwards. There was a fire in the fireplace and my head hit the coal and my hair burned a little before Papa could pull me out. I guess you could say I was a little hard headed and fast because Satan was always trying to take me out, But God.

One night my cousins Pake, Sputnik and I were getting our lesson on the floor next to the Kerosene lamp, it didn't have a glove on it so the flame was just out there. The weather was cool but not really cold. I had a long sleeve flannel gown on and I kept swishing my gown over the lamp almost putting out the flame, with my cousins telling me to sit down and Papa told me too. But I had to do it one more time. Guess what? My gown caught fire.

Sputnik said, "Huh! Monk your gown on fire." I looked back and saw the flames. Then I started running as they were telling me to stop. Papa caught me as I was about to jump off the top step, smothered the flame with a quilt and wrapped me up. I didn't get burned at all on my skin. But God.

The Lord was making a way for my grandparents to be able to take care of their families and preparing the way for me and my mom when we came back home. Even though my dad was not with me, God made away anyway. He also brought my grandma a new bedroom set for her guest room, we called it the front room. He also bought her a dining room set including table and chairs and a safe for her dishes.

She had a nice place to sleep for visitors and a nice place for them to eat also. This was all brought the year before I was born, in 1944. I still have the Chiffon and the safe. My dad is still with me. When my mom turned 62, she decided to put in for her social security check. When she applied for it she wasn't going to get much for being on father's farm. They asked her about marriage and she told them. They asked her if she wanted to know where he was, she said, she didn't care.

They asked if there were any children. She said yes and told them about me. They called and asked me if I wanted them to look for him and it wouldn't cost me anything. Boy was I happy. This was the year of 1985. It didn't take long, they called me back and said that he passed away in 1972. He

14

was buried in Arlington Cemetery in Kentucky by a man friend. We thought maybe he had remarried because I had received a letter from a girl in 1964 saying she was 13-years old and my daddy's daughter.

Her name was Elizabeth Virginia. The letter was mailed to my grandparents' old address that they had during the time my dad was around. I tried to get in touch with her but I couldn't. The social security said, he hadn't been married anymore which meant my mom could draw from his social security. He had a good amount of money in it. My mom got all the back pay for six months for them finding out all the information. She also received a widower's pension each month for 10 years.

God used my dad to make a way for mom after all those years and for me because I didn't have to take care of my mom - she helped me. She helped me with my children, grandchildren and my husband in the times that we needed it. My mom found out she had cancer in 1993.

# Chapter 2

---

## ~Skills taught by mama~

Mama taught me how to cook, clean, wash, iron, sew, and quilt. We had to do all this before we could say we had a boyfriend. The first time I cooked cornbread the dogs wouldn't even eat it. You see, we ground our corn into a meal, so it was a plain meal. We also used plain flour, so we had to add baking powder, baking soda and salt in the meal to make it rise. When I made my cornbread, I didn't put enough baking powder so it didn't rise.

It was packed so tight you couldn't even break the bread. I also cooked peas, okra and chicken. Everything was good except the bread. Nobody talked about the bread but my youngest uncle said to my mom, "Keep Monk out of the kitchen."

I cried but Mama didn't stop there. She said, you learn from your mistakes. But God. I was 11 years old, when I made a good biscuit. Emma and Mama started me making biscuits. She had a boil under her arm so she couldn't make the dough.

When we washed we had to build a fire around a big black pot outside to boil water. We either had to carry the water from the spring, go get it from the creek or catch it in barrels when it rained. We had to wash the clothes in the tub or on a rubboard then boil the clothes in the pot after we got hot water to wash. After boiling we had to wash again on the rubboard then rinse twice in tubs of clear water. If the men's overalls were really dirty we had to beat them with a batting stick on a block of wood after the first wash and before boiling. We beat the dirt out.

One day I wanted to go into town and they said, I could go if I washed Papa's overalls. I washed those overalls just like I knew how to do. I put them on a clothesline and was getting ready to go to town that afternoon. It was a summer day in June. The day was hot so it didn't take long for the overalls to dry. Mama went to check the overalls just as I was getting ready to leave. Guess what? I couldn't go to town because the overalls weren't clean. I had to rewash the overalls plus I had to carry water from the spring to wash twice, boil and rinse twice. You know what? I don't half wash anything to this day.

We didn't have electricity. So, to iron, we had to heat our heavy iron by fire. We had good oak wood that would heat real good. Regardless of the season, Mama would starch pillowcases and top sheets, anything that went on the company bed. We had to press everything including "t-shirts" and boxers. We would clean the irons with green pine straws in the fireplace to keep from getting black smudges on the white shirts. We also had to damp wet cloth to wipe the shirts so it wouldn't leave a spot that we called a "cat face."

Quilting was fun. I love piecing a quilt together. All the women would meet at one house after they were out from the field to quilt. When I was old enough and could reach the quilting frame, I started quilting. I got different patterns from our next-door cousin. The easy pattern was called string quilting. When I got married the first time, I had seven quilts.

When I was in middle school I had to come home and cook. Mama and Papa farmed but they let us go to school. The boys had to go to the field after school. I had to stay home, cook and bring in water from the spring. If I didn't bring enough for cooking, bathing and enough for the night we would have to go to the spring before going to school. I only had my cousin to help me and she was 8 years younger.

We had to carry in wood for the wood stove in the summer to cook mornings and to heat water for baths. One day Mama told me to come home, kill a chicken, go to the garden and get turnip greens. Now the chicken we ate was kept on a floored pen and was fed corn. She said kill that chicken right there; it was a red one. When Mama said that chicken, she meant that chicken, and not any other. When I got home I made a fire in the wood stove to heat the water so I could pick and clean the chicken.

Guess what? The chicken got out. Me and my cousin ran the chicken over that hill until it got tied up in a corner and we caught it. That was the longest day because you could see that chicken all day during class to make sure I didn't kill the wrong one. Then I had to go to the garden and pick the turnips, carry them to the spring with a tub to wash them. Turnips can get really grit with dirt so I had to wash them three-four times to get them clean. It was easier for me to carry them to the spring than it was for me to carry that much water to the house.

I picked, cleaned and cooked the chicken, cooked the turnips greens, cornbread and made ice tea. I also still had to get the water and wood in for the night; then churn butter with my little cousin's help. She was short and fat but a hard worker. I know this was hard work but Mama and Papa did let us go to school to get an education. Many children couldn't go to school or had to miss a lot of days but we could go as long as we worked after school and on Saturday's.

# Chapter 3

---

## ~Skills taught by papa~

Papa was a wise old man who taught us by parables. He didn't use the words "do and don't" often, but he would use parables and then would ask which one do you think is right. Another phrase he would use was, "you just be right." He'd tell us not to worry about the other person. He also taught us that if we get an education that's good but if we become a dishwasher or a street cleaner be the best. Be so good so when people see you they will say you know that lady or man is the best dishwasher or street cleaner.

Papa couldn't read or write anything, but he knew how to sign his name. You couldn't figure him out though. When we had algebra, he could get the answer but not like we could and neither could, we understand his way but the answer would be correct.

He was a smart farmer also, he planted cotton and made as much or more than any person around. He didn't use poison to keep the boo evil away. Everybody wanted to know how we did it, both blacks and whites.

He said, "I planted it and left it to God."

I didn't know we were poor until after I was grown. Papa kept a truck and it had to be a Chevrolet. He made a little house for the back so he could take people to town on Saturday that didn't have transportation for a small fee. Mostly people out of Monterey, a little place approximately 4 miles from where we lived.

We were never really hungry, we didn't have what we wanted all the time but we always had food. Papa not only planted corn and cotton, but he had a large garden with collard greens, turnips greens, mustard greens, different peas and beans, okra, white and sweet potatoes and onions for us to eat. He also planted peanuts, cucumbers, watermelon, tomatoes, peppers and sugar cane. He raised our hogs, cows, chickens and at one time goats. We had peaches, plums, apples, pears, blueberries and pomegranates.

We had so much in the garden we practically ate greens year-round. We canned some peas, beans, okra, tomatoes and corn. We didn't have a freezer back then. We canned for days. We could keep all the dry peas and beans for winter. We had a big loft in that old house so we kept them up there. Papa made a big bank that kept the potatoes underground. He made cane syrup and sorghum syrup. He kept it in one room of the barn in large barrels. He would kill 3 to 4 hogs a year. We had a smokehouse to smoke the ham. We had shoulders, sausages, bacon and crackling. We would salt the salt meat in barrels.

The chickens stayed ready to kill when needed. We had other chickens that laid eggs. We made corn into a meal. We only bought flour, sugar, flavoring, black pepper, salt, bologna, fish or sometimes we'd go fishing. We got the milk from the cows and we churn for buttermilk and butter.

Papa didn't believe in debt unless it was something important and it was important to keep your word. He didn't live with insurance. He said he could save just as well as they could and he did. When Mama died, he had enough to pay for her funeral. Before she died, she had to have both of her legs removed because of diabetes. He took care of her. And he had enough for his funeral also.

# Chapter 4

---

## ~*School*~

One other thing Papa did, we had to buy our books when we were in school. We worked in the field before school started when the cotton crop was good. He would have to hire help so he would pay us half the price of what he paid those he hired.

High school years were great. I was an honor student mainly because my cousin who was two grades ahead of me was very smart, especially in Math and Science helped me. I was the first female to finish school in my family and my cousin was the first male. We made our family proud. My youngest uncle was eight years older; he quit in the 11th grade. My oldest first cousin was 4 years older and he quit in the 6th grade. He stayed in trouble at school. He followed behind my uncle even leaving home at an early age.

I was popular in high school with the boys. I had many boyfriends. I also had many girlfriends but only two are still a part of my life. My best friend and I met when I was 11. She was 8 months older than me. I studied two grades in one year so I was equal with her. During high school my best friend could not go most places because her daddy was really strict. I would stay with her so she could go to the banquet, prom, etc. her daddy would take us and pick us up. I loved her parents, especially her mom. She also had an older sister, two younger sisters and three younger brothers.

They made me feel like I fit right in. I didn't have a sister or brother and I didn't have a dad either. I remember I spent the night with her for our 10th grade banquet so she could go. Her dad took us. We had made moonshine in chemistry class. The boys hid some and put it in the punch. We were all drunk. When we got home that night we had to climb these really high steps in order to get in the house. We had to brace each other up.

My best friend whispered to me and said, "Virginia, these steps are getting higher and higher."

I said, "You hush before your dad finds out and he won't carry us anywhere anymore." We laughed.

He said, "What's so funny?"

"Nothing," we said.

She wasn't real book smart but had what my parents would call a mother's wit. I would help her with her homework and beg her to do her lessons so she could get a passing grade. She taught me how to sew in home-economics and she also taught me how to curl my hair.

Guess what? We graduated in 1962! She was 17 and I was 16. There were no jobs for blacks in Greenville, only house work. The pay for house work was nothing, maybe $5.00 a day if the person was kind. All the girls were going off to college or to New York to get jobs. The work in New York was house work also, but you live in, eat, pay no rent and made $60.00 a week by your employer. That was big money back then.

So, I went to New York leaving my home to help my mom on the farm. I left for New York when I was 18. In between school and then, I helped my mom gather corn while Papa drove the wagon up and down the corn rows in the field. We broke and threw the corn on the wagon. We also stripped sugar cane and helped make syrup. After we had finished in the field, I began to piece quilts and quilted them along with my mom, grandma and cousin. During this winter I made seven quilts.

I had a cousin in town, we went fishing on good days or just visited each other. She left home before me. I was also seeing my boyfriend from time to time. His name was Johnathon. He was really popular, handsome and could sing. He wouldn't stay in one place long enough and I never knew where he was. He wouldn't keep a job so he always ended up back at his mom's house. His mom was a smart woman, and worked a farm that had hogs, cows and chickens. She raised twelve children, mostly without her husband's help.

When I saw that my boyfriend wasn't stable and wouldn't work, I decided to go to New York. I was going where my friend was, but as I was getting ready to go she was on her way home for vacation. So, I decided to go through an agency. I had to get a transcript from my principal, take my diploma and I had to attend school for three weeks to make sure we could clean. There were 16 girls in the class. The agency gave us a place to sleep but we had to buy our own food.

I cried from Montgomery all the way to New York. That was my first time leaving my mom for that long.

One of the ladies from the agency told me, "Please don't go back home, because if you do you won't ever leave your mom again."

I stayed. I did good for a country girl that went alone. We were given instructions to follow:

1.  Please don't take a cab to Rockville Center
2.  Take a cab to the subway and take the subway to Rockville Center
3.  Don't ask a stranger for directions, ask a policeman.

I did everything right even though I had to go to a couple of tracks before I got to the right one. I had two suitcases and a shoulder bag. My arms were so sore when I got to the Rockville Center. I took a cab to the agency. There were 15 more girls, some from Frisco City. They had taken the cab from the city and it took most of their money leaving them with little to eat off of. Papa gave me the money for my fare before I left and said whatever you do, don't spend this. If you get there and don't like it or the job doesn't work out you can always come home. Guess what? I used that money to come back home.

We had a dorm to sleep in but it was one large room with single beds. There were bathrooms for us to share and a little diner for us to eat. The food was good and I only had two meals a day to make my money last until I got a job without spending my fare. I was there three days before getting a job because everyone thought I was too young and too small. I only weighed 105 lbs. The third day a little old lady came in and asked questions about cleaning. The other girls were taller and bigger than I.

Her last question was who can iron white shirts? I raised my hand and I was the only one to raise my hand. The lady's name was Ms. Higgins.

She said, "I need someone who can iron white shirts but you look so little. You got the job." After I worked for one week, she said, "You iron better than the laundry and can clean also. You're a piece of leather but you are well put together." But God. Remember that the Holy Spirit leads and guides us into all truth and he always gives us what we need. My 7th grade teacher corrected me to clean well and my Mama made me iron clothes, especially the starched white shirts with the iron that had to be heated by the fire.

My first teacher taught me how to set the table and eat properly. I worked for Mr. and Ms. Higgins from July until November. I lived in their home on Long Island. They were great people. I made $65.00 a week and I didn't have to pay for anything except for my occasional outing. I had to take a cab to the bus stop. I could have walked but the first time I tried I had a bad experience. Just before getting on the bus I had to walk through an alley with no houses, when I got to the last house a car was following me.

The Holy Spirit told me not to go through the alley, so I turned around and circled the block with the car following me and calling out the window for me to ride with him. I was on my way to church. A lady was looking out her window and saw me. She called out, "circle again" and when I did the cops came and he left. She asked me into her house and I called Mr. Higgins. He came and picked me up. I was too scared to go to church so I went back home. From that time on I had the same cab pick me up and bring me home.

I didn't know that the Higgins had arranged for them to transport me and my fare was always the same. The cab drivers told me when they came to get me to take me to the bus stop to go home, But God.

I got ahead of myself again. In their home I had my own little apartment. I had a bedroom, a sitting room, bathroom and also a kitchenette with a small refrigerator where I could keep snacks. I had a TV and a radio. I lived in the basement. I was on one side; the utility room was in the center and Mr. Higgins kept all kinds of antique lamps on the other end. I met three girls that were working in the neighborhood but I don't even remember their names. I went out with them once and they went to a club when we were supposed to be going to a movie.

They were drinking and smoking. I got back home safe because one of the girls took me to the cab stand. I didn't go with them anymore. I met an older lady across the street and everyone called her Mom Betty. She kept three children for a young couple. She ran that household and accepted finances in some of that too; she was a native New Yorker. She had been married three times and had twenty-one children. Her husbands were dead and her children are all grown. Her baby boy was my age. She had her home and church in the city. She went home every Sunday morning.

Our days off were Thursday and Sunday. Mrs. Higgins first gave me Thursday and Saturday but when I learned that everybody else has Sunday instead of Saturday off I asked to switch Mom Betty took me home with her to introduce me to her son his name is Ernest. I had a cousin that lived in the city in the Bronx. She was my mother's first cousin who had gone to New York and hadn't been home. Her name was the same as my mom and she had a daughter named Jean. My mom's cousin didn't know me.

I went home with my Mom Betty on Thursday and her son took me sightseeing and took me to see my cousin; he left me there. She lived on the 16th floor of the apartment building. She had a big dinner cooked. It was a southern meal but she also had duck, my first-time having duck but their fried chicken, collard greens, okra, mac and cheese and sweet potato pie were like brother rabbit. "I was in a briar patch" back home with a southern meal. Her daughter was seven or eight and she was glad to have a cousin from the south.

She also was glad that we both were only children. Ernest came and got me around 4 o'clock and then went back to Mom Betty's until it was time for us to get on the subway to head back to the island. We went back to work. Mom Betty walked her dog every evening just before dark. When Mrs. Higgins cooked lamb chops or more than we could eat, I'd fix it up and give it to Mom Betty. Mom Betty would cook for the children but it would be things like hamburgers, hot dogs, spaghetti or something they would like to eat. She will cook a good dinner if the mom and dad were coming home for dinner which was once a week maybe.

I went back with Mom Betty on Sunday. I went to see my cousin again but I didn't stay long. Ernest took me sightseeing again then to Mom Betty's house. She fixed a good southern meal also but she didn't say southern she was a New Yorker she said, "This is nigger food." She had black eyed peas, cornbread, ham, candied yams, rice and tea. I don't like tea so I had a coke. We finished eating and went to church. I was surprised when we got there. I had asked Mom Betty about her religion but I knew she was a Christian. I thought she was Baptist, but she was holy, speaking in tongues and all. You wouldn't have known it being around her daily, no more than how kind, loveable and giving she was. But God.

The next week I got a letter from my mom. She was my friend while she was home on her vacation. She gave her address and phone number so when she got back to New York she called me. Oh, I was so happy but we were a good way apart. She worked in Sussex, Long Island. We made plans to meet in Hempstead, Long Island. The buses would change and go from one place to another for Hempstead. It was the largest town on the island.

On Thursday, I met Lil and I didn't know that she was going to have more girls with her. They were her sisters and two more girls from back home. We all went to a movie and out to eat. We went to the Apollo club twice to see James Brown and other singers. We were there when James Brown recorded 'Please, Please.' I got another letter from home. This time Emma was telling me that Johnathon had written to me and she sent me the letter. He wanted me to marry him.

You remember the young man I was seeing before I left home that was popular, could sing and wouldn't stay in one place long. Now he wants to get married. My mom was like please come home and get married, I don't want you to be in New York by yourself. I talked to Mom Betty being an older Christian woman, the answer would be yes. I talked to Lil and her sisters and they thought it was great. Lil's sister was to marry a man from her home also. They graduated together. He was in the army so she worked until he came home. I told Mrs. Higgins and she said ok.

I worked until the weekend before Thanksgiving then I went and stayed overnight with Lil where she worked. She went with me to get my ticket and get on the bus. Oh, before that Lil went shopping with me to get a dress for me to get married in. It was a short knee length white gown, gathered at the waist with long sleeves. Lil made my veil. Mom Betty bought me a pretty gray dress with red stripes to wear after the wedding. Mrs. Higgins gave me a silver bread tray. I got ahead of myself again while working, I bought shoes with a purse to match.

I had black, beige, white, brown, red and navy blue with outfits to match also. I had boots and a heavy coat too. Mrs. Higgins taught me to knit a beautiful mohair white sweater. My mom didn't know and washed the sweater in hot water. It turned out like a doll sweater. Mrs. Higgin's daughter gave me a fox stove. I had saved money and wanted to buy everyone a gift back home. I wanted to get my little cousin a dress because I named her. I went back home with $25 my granddad had given me to keep for my fare back home. I bought my ticket with it. I rode the greyhound bus. I left New York on Thursday evening and didn't get to Greenville, AL until Saturday morning. Long ride, huh? While I was on the bus I saw a man reading the paper on the seat in front of me which stated that John F. Kennedy was assassinated. I was really shocked.

When I left home they had started desegregation. When I got home, we did not have a bus station so I had to get off at the filling station. My mom, Papa, aunt and uncle were waiting for me. We went downtown shopping and I bought everybody something.

I was so glad to see my mom and family. My mom, Emma hugged me and cried. When I got home I told Mama thanks again for teaching me to wash, sew, and iron. Then I started making my wedding plans. I was getting married on Christmas, which was a month away. I went to see my cousins on the hill. They had a little store at the end of their backyard. She was like my spiritual mom. She and her husband told me they would make my wedding cake and they did.

They made a 3-tier cake with the bride and groom on top. It was homemade and delicious. They also gave me a 4-piece place setting of dishes. I am the oldest granddaughter so Papa wanted to give me a big wedding and he did. He also had it announced on the Boogie man. The Boogie man was a man that played blues every afternoon on the radio and he would make announcements for you when you write in and tell him. Papa asked me to write to Boogie man to announce our wedding on Christmas day at 3 o'clock.

Papa didn't like spending money or you could say that he was stingy but he re-floored the kitchen and did something

I had never known him to do. He got smiley vines to put all around the porch with holly branches with red berries every few feet. He helped me get Christmas decorations for the tree, it was tall and bib. He didn't complain about buying the food to cook for the wedding. Mama, Emma, my aunt and I made cakes, pies, salads, dressing, fried chicken, ham and turkey. Neighbors and friends donated food.

There were so many people. Everyone couldn't park on the hill. We got married on the front porch. The weather was nice, the sun was shining and it wasn't cold. Lil was my maid of honor and a friend of Johnathon was his best man.

His nephew married us. He was a few years younger and hadn't been preaching long. We stayed at home the first night and I was so embarrassed the next morning to face my mom and grandparents with my aunt teasing. I was a virgin and boy what a night. We knocked over the Christmas tree. I was running on my back and must have kicked it over. The next night we stayed with his mom and got up the next day and headed to Cleveland, OH.

His older brother and his wife were home for Christmas so his mom paid for us to go back with them. I didn't know this at the time. I thought Johnathon was paying for our expenses. Then when we got to Cleveland, we stayed with the oldest brother and wife but he had another brother and his wife staying there. The oldest brother was buying so the other brother rented two bedrooms on the second floor. Everyone shared the first floor: living room, den, dining room, kitchen, basement with washer and dryer, the other brother let us use the second bedroom on the second floor.

We were supposed to get the third floor which had two bedrooms and a separate living area. I didn't know this until later. Jonathan knew but I didn't. We had been there three months before the other brother's wife began telling me that Johnathon wasn't paying them any rent and that he was supposed to move on the third floor. She needed her room because her brother and sister were coming for the summer. Then I found out that I was pregnant. I didn't have a job because no one was taking the time to teach me the bus routes that would take me to get job applications. I couldn't drive and neither could his brother's wife. She had been there sometimes and was a chef at a motel. The oldest brother's wife did house work like I did but she didn't help.

Jonathan left one day looking for a job and didn't come home that evening or next. There I was pregnant with no money. They did feed me because I was pregnant. Then after he was gone a week the other brother's wife told me I had to get out of her room because she needed it. So, there I was pregnant with nowhere to go, no money and no husband. But God. The young sister had been there one day and she gave me her number. She said if you need me, call me. She knew Johnathon had disappeared.

The Holy Spirit brought this to mind but then I didn't know about the Holy Spirit. I called the younger sister and told her what happened and she said, "ok, I'll be there as soon as my husband gets off work."

I had packed our things and cleaned up my sister in law's room. I waited downstairs for the younger sister in law. She was a few years younger. I married a man that was 16 years older. The younger sister was big boned, nicely built so she could've been mistaken for 18 to 20.

I cried all day long because in three months I was pregnant, no job, no husband, no money and nowhere to stay. I was too ashamed to tell my mom.

I had said to her before we married, "do you think Johnathon is going to do the disappearing act after we get married?"

39

She said, "no, look at all his brothers, they are taking care of their families."

I went home with their younger sister and husband. I had to sleep on the couch but it was big enough. Most of all they made me feel welcome. The tears didn't stop though because I felt I had failed in my marriage. My brother in law was a chef at a motel also. He had been one in Pensacola and his job transferred him to Cleveland. He could really cook so my sister in law and I didn't cook because he didn't think it was good enough.

I was there two weeks before Johnathon came. He slept on the couch with me for a week. He had a little money so his sister told him to rent the front apartment in the building where they stayed, they had the back one. It had a bedroom, living room, small kitchen and bathroom. They were already furnished and only cost $15 weekly. There were no utility bills. The landlord lived next door.

Jonathan paid for two weeks but told me he paid for the month. He stayed for a week and a few days. Guess what? He disappeared again leaving me thinking I was good for two more weeks. I had half a loaf of bread, ½ jar of jelly, ½ stick of butter and ½ glass of milk. I stayed up front for a week and didn't tell my sister in law. I ate a butter, jelly sandwich two times a day with a ½ glass of milk for a week and I was three months pregnant. But God.

She went to pay her rent and the lady asked where her brother was with his rent. So, she came to see. I told her he had been gone for a week.

She looked in the refrigerator and said, "You should be ashamed of myself for not telling us."

There I was again crying my eyes out, reading my bible and writing my mom letters telling her everything but I would not mail them because I know she would walk to Cleveland. We lived on Carnegie Ave. It was six lanes wide. When I got tired of reading, crying and writing, I would count the cars. My sister in law took me down to see the landlord and she told me that my husband had only paid for two weeks instead of a month. She said she could just look at him and tell he was a liar and a lady's man. She let me stay there.

I told her I would write to my mom and get her money but my sister in law had a friend. She introduced him to me and he would take us out to eat. We began talking and he was from Selma, AL. I told him that's where my father was from. He didn't know him but he said his wife loved handmade quilts. I made seven quilts before I got married. I pieced them by hand and my mom and cousin from down the road helped me quilt them.

He bought two for $100 each. But God. I had to keep one to sleep under. I paid the rent back and went and got food. Yes! Then I had to get some clothes because at this point nothing was fitting me. I didn't tell my mom that I had sold the quilts and I didn't tell her about my husband. I stayed at the apartment, making plans to go home.

Another sister in law had four children, two girls and two boys. The boys were older. The baby was crawling but not walking. Anyway, she wanted to go to work to help her husband financially. She asked me to keep the kids and she would give me $25 a week.

I said, "okay," because my plan was to work until June, keep my apartment and then go home. I enjoyed keeping the children and doing a little house work. Her husband was really nice too. Everybody's husband was except mine. While I was watching her kids, I had to pass a fish market and there was a red snapper in the window I would stop and look at. One day the man saw me looking and gave it to me dressed and ready to cook because I was pregnant.

In May, I learned that the oldest brother was going home in June. I asked if he would bring me and he said yes for $50. I know he thought I didn't have it. But God.

Then he said, "does your husband know?" Acting as he didn't know he was gone.

I said, "it's okay, I can get the bus."

But his wife said, "yes, Virginia, you can go with us because you might be a little safer with us. I wrote and told Emma I was coming home in June to stay and have my baby. She sent me some money. I went and got a bigger 2-piece dress and a pair of brown loafer shoes to wear home. Oh! Before I went home, my sister in law that I was working for took me to the doctor. I hadn't seen a doctor for almost seven months. Well, I was seven months old at the time of the exam.

The doctor was black, young and handsome. I was scared out of my wits. He had to sit and talk to me to calm me down. When he found out that I had lived in New York he began talking to me about being there and my marriage. He finally got the job done and told me that I had a fine, healthy baby boy. But God. My sister and brother in law paid the doctor bill.

I still didn't know where my husband was and I made it back home in June. I was glad to be back on the hill with everyone. I was home for a week when Emma decided to take me to the doctor. The doctor was the only OB-GYN in Greenville. He was a good doctor, white and old. My mother in law paid for all my doctors' visits. The doctor told me that my baby was healthy but could put on a little weight, but he then said he can do that after he gets out.

I stayed from one house to the other even though my mother in law wanted me to stay with her all the time. She was trying to make up for what her son wasn't doing. I went to the doctor the 1st of August and he said the baby would be born the last of August or the 1st of September. I went to stay with my mother for a week then my back began to hurt. So, I sent a note to my youngest sister in law to give to my cousin. They were both in the 12th grade and neither family had a phone.

My cousin drove my mom over to get me after he got home from school. Mother wanted me to go but I wasn't taking a chance of my baby being born at her house. Nothing against her, I just wanted my Emma, Mama, my aunt and cousins. My back began to hurt me so badly Emma took me to the doctor. It was the morning of August 31st. He told Emma to take me home and that I would be having the baby no later than 4 o'clock that afternoon. We came home that afternoon and Papa said that gal is not going to have that baby this early because it's her first one.

She could be lingering around for days but he didn't know that I had been at mom's house. Oh, the tears started again and I still hadn't heard from Johnathon. I was fixing to have our baby. The midwife had to be paid. The baby would need milk, clothes and need to see the doctor. Everyone is telling me to stop crying because everything is going to be alright. Later on, in the day the pains begin to get worse. Mama used to be good with the birthing of babies but she was old and not in good health.

Emma was scared because this was my first child and I was her only child. One reason is because one of our cousins' wife from down the road had died during childbirth. She was only a few years older than me. I told my aunt to send someone to get my spiritual mother. She only came up that hill when someone was sick or to quilt. She came up that hill to examine me and told Papa that the doctor was right, "because Jim this baby is coming."

He still said, "ahh, you all don't know what you're talking about."

She told me, baby don't worry, just do what I tell you to do. She said, "believe in God, we are going to have this baby." She got on the foot of the bed and said push. I pushed when she told me to. Then she said, "here comes the head." They told me she said Emma ran all the way down to the spring. The next thing she said was, "that's my girl, by the grace of God we have a healthy baby boy. Jim, now go get the midwife."

She couldn't do the rest because she didn't have a license.

Papa said, "well, I'll be doggone. I thought this gal wouldn't have this baby so soon."

He was born right at 4 o'clock. He was right on time then and still loves to be on time. He was healthy but I couldn't nurse him, my milk wasn't any good. He didn't have to have the expensive milk though. Through it all a healthy baby boy, no husband and no job. My plans were to go back to New York after Christmas. My mother in law was still helping me out. She gave us things from her farm to help feed us.

September, October and November still, there was no Johnathon. The baby was growing and doing all the things that babies do at that age. I shared those moments with my mom and family. Tears still began to come. Then on Christmas morning when we all were sitting around the fireplace, children playing on the floor. Emma, my aunt and I were in the kitchen around the wood stove fixing breakfast for the children. Then there was a knock on the door.

We were a little shocked because everyone used the back door, which opens most of the time because the sun rose on that side of the house. So, my cousin opened the door and said Johnathon. There he was with boxes, bags and groceries. Everyone went and spoke to him and said how glad they were to see him. I was speechless, no words would come.

He was like, "Ginger, I'm home…" I was like, I see. Then he picked up Jr. and he was crying and going on. Little that I knew, that once again he came home broke and mother had borrowed money for her and the kids to make it through winter and used some to bail him out again.

My friend Lillie wanted me to name the baby Elliot but I went on and named him Jr. which didn't hurt him one bit. They were thinking I wasn't going to name him Jr. because I was mad, but still did it. Jonathan came in with gifts for me, Mama and Jr. he had everything in the line of food. He bought flour, meal, sugar, grits, rice, canned goods, all kinds of meats and anything you can think of. Oh, he was crying and apologizing to my mom and Papa about leaving his responsibilities on them. He even gave Papa the money back he paid the midwife, which was $25.00.

He stayed home for a long while this time, he would come over to the house everyday trying to get me to go back to his mom's house with him. I wouldn't go because I hadn't gotten over the hurt. Papa kept talking to me saying he believes he is going to do better because every time he would come over he would bring some type of grocery item. You see, Papa didn't like buying groceries so that was money he was saving. I still wouldn't go.

One of my classmates was getting married so he asked me to go to the wedding with him. Emma and my aunt talked me into going. After the wedding we went to Mother's house and she was talking to us and asking me to come back to Johnathon because of the baby. She said we could stay with her until we got our own place. Since Papa was after me too, I gave in and went back. Plus, I loved the man.

Jonathan begins working. I had to get up every morning to get the fire going in that wood stove.

I would say, "Johnathon, get up and start the fire."

Mother would say, "he has to work hard all day. Why can't you do it? Because you ain't using my electric stove."

I would get up and make a fire, cook biscuits, sausage, eggs and then I would fix his lunch. The first day I didn't fix enough for Mother, her two sons and daughters. So, she went in there and cooked them something on the electric stove. That evening she told me to help with dinner on the wood stove.

I did, after we cooked she said, "you need to go get splinters to start the fire in the morning so Johnathon won't be late."

Jonathan comes home, takes a bath and talks to the neighbors. As you notice with all my doing no one helped me with the baby. Jonathan's sister would play with him a little when I was with Emma. I told them about the way things were.

Papa was like, "huh? You are just being spoiled, being the only child and all."

I just kept my mouth closed. Three weeks later Johnathon was tired of the job and said a friend of his had a job for him in Birmingham. So, he left to go to Birmingham.

I was going back home and Mother said, "stay with me until he sends for you."

Some daughter in laws stayed with their mother in laws all the time, especially if the husbands were working out of town. I stayed with Mother because I was under the influence that the responsibility would be on Papa.

A month later Johnathon sent two friends of ours that he was staying with in Birmingham and said for me to come back with them. He had an Apartment in the building with them and a job with them. Since we were all reared up in Forest Home I begin to think okay maybe he will do right this time around since we all knew each other. The landlord was a real nice lady and would feed Jr. his breakfast every morning.

He loved oatmeal and would play on the blanket all day. She would keep him until I clean, wash and cook. Or while I walked to the store with the lady I knew in the building. Jonathan was doing good or so I thought. I wanted to work and the landlady had agreed to keep Jr.

Jonathan said, "No." He did not want that lady to keep his baby. Then he got to the point where he did not want me going anywhere with the lady. He then said don't go believe anything they told you.

I thought, "here we go again…" I began to feel bad. It was eight weeks we were there. I found out I was pregnant again. Jonathan left that weekend and did not return. When he didn't come home that Monday, the landlord told me that he hadn't paid rent in two weeks. She said he just kept lying to her making excuses. The couple began telling me things. Then they said we brought you up here, we are taking you home.

I said, "Okay, I would appreciate it."

I didn't have any money to give for gas but they said that was okay. I went back to Emma and Papa very disappointed and didn't say anything. I had one baby and was pregnant with another. Mother to cover for Johnathon, sent me to Dr. Dunklin with a note telling him to charge everything to her, but I didn't stay with her anymore.

My Mama's baby sister asked me, Emma and Jr to come stay with her for two weeks in Pensacola. She lived in Brent with her friend Fred. They had bought an acre of land with a trailer on it. They had two bedrooms and they let us sleep in the larger one. I went to Dr. Dunklin before I left and he said it would be okay for me to go. We went down there so we could spend the 4th of July. My cousin was sending my aunt money every month and told her to use some for us. We were there for a week, we had been to see the other aunts and uncles.

On the 12th of July, I got up to use the bathroom and my water broke. It was only my 7th month. They teased me about the baby not wanting to be born in Alabama with a midwife. My aunt didn't have a car that day so she called my uncle. He came from downtown to take me to the hospital in a '49 Ford. It was an old car and was very hot but got us there. My aunt had to pay $50 to get me in Escambia General. My cousin had just sent that money to her. Emma told her she would give it back after talking to Papa.

Emma told Papa to sell a cow so she could have money to pay her sister back and help us while we were with her. Sister was born. She was very small weighing 2 lbs. and 10 ounces. Then she fell all the way down to 1 lbs. 14 ounces. We thought for sure she wasn't going to make it. But God! I told my Mama to tell my spiritual mom and she did. Then Sister began gaining weight, about 2 ounces every day. She had to weigh 5 lbs. before they would let her out of the hospital.

Our two weeks turned into one month. But God! You see if I had been home with a midwife she probably wouldn't have made it. Papa didn't send any money so my uncle had to pay $50 for us to get her out. Guess what? Her daddy was down there staying with his aunt. He came over crying again but he had the right one then.

My aunt said, "cut out the tears, come and sign for this bill."

He brought Jr. some milk and food. Also, Emma snuff. The doctor said Sister was healthy. Like usual, I couldn't keep in touch with Johnathon. One day he came out to see us and Fred's cousin was there. He swore that he was there to see me. I didn't see that because I hadn't got Johnathon out of my system. We went back home with Sister and promises from her daddy. Sister had to have SMA milk and back then it was $1.10 a can. It was good she couldn't drink a lot.

My cousin and aunt helped again. She would put clothes on Layaway and send them to me at Christmas time. My cousin would send money every month. Jonathan came home again when Sister was three months old. He came with milk, clothes and food again. He did it for about two months. Papa kept telling me to go back to his mom's house. It was worse this time. But I told Papa I am going back but this the last time, and I will give him six weeks and he will be gone and I will be pregnant.

If I am, I am coming back here and you are going to take care of us and pay for the baby to be born. You see God had another child for me to have by him. I went back and he went back to work where he used to again with his friend's dad. He was making more money this time. He got tired of the job again in two weeks. He went back to Pensacola saying he would come home every two weeks. He got another job because he had to pay that hospital bill. His aunt said he couldn't come home every two weeks and pay the bills there.

I caught chicken pox and was very sick. Mother's brother came over one day and when he came she was reading her bible while I had both babies sitting on the dining room floor. I was outside the door washing diapers.

Her brother said, "Virginia, you are sweating with fever. You don't need to be doing this." He went inside and spoke to his sister and said, "I dare you to sit here and read your bible while this child is sick and washing babies' diapers."

I was able to wash them and hang them on the line. My sister in law came over that evening and took the diapers off the line for me when she saw that I had a temperature. I sent a note to Emma. Mother didn't know I sent the note. And when they came that evening Mother was like Ginger don't have to go, we can take care of the children.

After the chicken pox I went back and did not hear from Johnathon and he didn't come home. Mother was like why aren't you satisfied? You have a place to sleep and food to eat. I told her that I didn't marry her. So, I wrote a note to Papa and saying look it is eight weeks and Johnathon is still not here and I am pregnant. I am coming home and after this one, I am not going back even if I have to take all three of them and eat dirt in the swamps until we all die. Papa didn't argue. He just said okay.

I tried to work in Greenville. I would ride with one of my cousins who worked at the hospital. I only worked one day because the lady was scared to work with me because I might get hurt. God's way is not always easy and when I needed strength I would just call on the name of Jesus.

I always tell my children and grands, "you make your decisions, you make your mistakes. No one else makes it for you."

I took a wrong turn when I left New York because my mom didn't want me up there by myself. So, I talked myself into coming home because I knew I loved Johnathon and if I came home and got married my mom would feel better about it.

I kept saying, "but Emma, he's always disappearing during our courtship. He would be gone for months and I wouldn't hear from him or know where he was." My goal was to stay in New York and go to school like many of my friends.

So here I am again at Dr. Dunklin because my new baby was in a hurry. I got back in the bed with Jr. and Sister. Emma and my aunt fixed the bed under me with old quilts so I wouldn't mess the mattress up. My aunt caught my baby and she said this is my baby, my boy. I named him Tony. Papa teased her about doing more hollering then I was doing. Papa and my cousin went to get the midwife. My aunt had done everything right when she got there to cut the cord with Mama's help.

We didn't send to get my spiritual mom that night but she came over the next day. Papa thought he was finished with doctor bills. He thought he was only going to have to buy milk. Thank God that Tony could take the PET milk like Jr. but when he was a few days old he had problems with his eyes. Emma and my aunt had to take him to Dr. Douglas. He was the only doctor in Greenville that was kind to black people and would let them pay in time if they didn't have the money right then. Papa wasn't having that, he gave Emma the $15.00 to take him.

The first medicine we had didn't work so we took Tony back but this time Papa wanted to use home remedies.

I said, "not in my baby's eyes!"

He gave the doctor the money and the next medicine was expensive. The doctor said that if this medicine did not clear his eyes up then he would have to send him to Montgomery. I went home and took Tony to my spiritual mom and she prayed over his eyes. The next day all the puss kept running out. Tony would cry a lot so we had to hold him. We held him anyway to keep that stuff from running down his face. The next day his eyes were clear.

My aunt said, "Golly, no wonder it took them so long to clear up as big as they are." They were big but pretty eyes.

I hadn't seen Johnathon since he left me at Mother's. I guess she told him I was pregnant after I had the baby. I didn't tell him. Mother came with milk and groceries for the kids.

She said, "Ginger, you can come stay with me some."

I said, "Okay."

This was the last of September in the year of 1966. I said, "well, Lord you wanted me to have these three children." I tried to work in Greenville, but I didn't have the transportation. So, I wrote my aunt, the one who lives in Pensacola and asked if I could come work down there. She told me yes. She and her son had been helping me all along. He left home and went to Pensacola to work after he graduated. The year I got married, he went into the Air Force. He would send me money every month when he got paid. It was always just in time. People thought we were sister and brother.

It was Christmas. I prayed for Johnathon to come home for Christmas like he did in '64. My plan was to get him to stand and shoot Papa's pistol until it was empty. Well, God did not answer that prayer. Jonathan did not come home; but Mother came and she brought fruits, candy, toys and groceries. The man Papa rented from would come around and give the children fruit, candy and toys. He gave the grown people fruit and a piece of money. He did this for everyone that lived on his property.

My family had been on his land for so long that he just let them stay for nothing. Papa had land, but he would never build on it. My aunt and uncle had been writing to me telling me that his cousin had been asking about me and asked for me to come down there. He said he would take care of me and my children. I thought he was talking about another cousin of his that I had met. He was a nice guy and not bad looking.

Emma kept saying maybe he is talking about uncle Lawrence with the pretty smile. That's his cousin too. I said it doesn't make any difference because I was not going looking for a man. I wrote Jonathon and mailed it to his aunt's address because I heard he was still in Pensacola. I wrote to tell him not to try to see me or my children because I was finished. I also told him about what I planned to do to him but God didn't answer my prayer. I told him that Papa wasn't going to talk me into coming back to him anymore because Jonathon had told me that if I left Papa is going to make you come back.

So, there I was with three children. Living with my grandparents, my mom, my aunt and her six children. It was the year of 1967, and I decided to leave home. My aunt and uncle came and got me. I told Papa to let my children stay with Emma and that he wouldn't have to take care of them, I would. I didn't get on welfare. I didn't have a decent pair of shoes to take with me.

My cousin had a brand-new pair of loafers and she said to me, "I am going to let you have my damn shoes and when you get a job I want something back." I said okay and gave her a big hug.

When I got to my aunts, it seemed like every man in the neighborhood was coming around to talk to me. Most of them did not work, they just walked the streets drinking beer. It was April before I started working. I began working for a lady named Mrs. White, three days a week. I worked Monday, Wednesday, and Friday for $5 a day, from 9 in the morning until 3 in the afternoon. I would give my aunt $5.00 and I would send $10.00 to Emma.

I worked for Mrs. White, for three weeks before getting a job at a laundry on Davis Highway and Brent Lane. I made $25.00 every week. That was $10.00 more a week. Now I gave my aunt $10.00, sent Emma $10.00 and kept $5.00 for myself. With my $5 dollars, I got myself and my children insurance for $2.50 and I would put clothes on Layaway. I would babysit sometimes so I could catch the bus to Greenville to see them every two weeks. I could've applied for better jobs, but I couldn't drive.

Right next to where I worked they built a McDonalds. We could get a hamburger for *25* cents, fries for *10* cents and a coke for *5* cents. The job lasted for 4 months and then the laundry closed down. I went home to see my children. Tony wouldn't have anything to do with me at first. That really hurt, but he was only six months old when I left. After the cleaners closed, I got a job with a state trooper and his wife. I worked five days a week for *$25.00* weekly.

My uncle's cousin came to their home one Friday evening. I was washing dishes when Lawrence came in and he asked my aunt, "what mean little girl you have washing the dishes?"

She said, "that's no little girl Lawrence, that's my niece that has the baby down here remember?" *I think he knew already because his cousin had told him I was here.*

"I am not mean," I said, "I just mean what I say."

He said, "I like that…"

The next day he came out again. He had my aunt keeping his money so he would come get some. He started a conversation and he asked me out, after he asked me if I knew how to make biscuits. I wasn't going to go out with him, but my aunt said I should, so I did. We seemed to hit it off from the beginning. I did something I thought I would never do, especially on a first date, but remember I was married, separated for over a year, had three children and was twenty-two years old.

Lawrence was handsome, a smooth operator and said everything I needed to hear. Lawrence, my uncle and aunt talked me into drinking a beer because I missed my children and wasn't sleeping at night. I started drinking whatever Lawrence would drink, but not as much. I would go out to the clubs with him even though I didn't want to because I wanted to please him. I was always scared. I couldn't stand the cursing and fighting that went on in the clubs.

I grew up in church, believing in God and trusting Him for all my needs. That was how I made it this far with three children and an unfaithful husband. I didn't turn away from God, but I was serving two masters. I began feeling displeased with myself. So, in the year of '68, I told Lawrence he was going to move out from the lady he was staying with and get a place of his own and we both have to get a divorce.

Lawrence's granddaddy died. I went to Monroeville with my aunt and uncle because that was his uncle. We stayed all night. Lawrence was with his lady friend or was supposed to be. They stayed at Lawrence's mothers house. He had told everyone about me. I met Lawrence's mother, but she only knew me as my aunt's niece. I met his brother, his oldest sister and her husband. He told everyone I was a nurse. I guess because I said I would like to be one.

His baby sister was still in high school. He had nine brothers and two sisters. He also had lots of nieces and nephews which were crazy about him. He was always looked up to by many of his brothers and his dad also.

Lawrence and I had gone out for three years. He was everything I wanted in a man and husband. Or so I thought. I knew he would love to go out and dance, drink and gamble, but I thought I could change all that. I thought if I could get back in church Lawrence would eventually come with me. I knew all of his brothers that were married in Monroeville were unfaithful to their wives, but not Lawrence.

Lawrence finally moved out of the house with the lady. He was still close friends with his wife's brother, he helped him move into an apartment downtown. He had one big room with a bed, dresser, kitchen in one corner and sitting room in the middle. The bathroom was at the end of the hall and was shared by two or more couples. That was craziness. Lawrence would have to stand at the door while I went to the bathroom. I got my divorce, but Lawrence was stalling getting his saying his wife wouldn't give him one.

I told him if he didn't we couldn't see each other anymore and I would go back home because I could not live this way any longer. He got a divorce.

Everyone started telling me about Lawrence's lifestyle other than drinking, dancing and gambling. They said he had affairs with women and how he would beat them. Every time I asked Lawrence he would deny it. His cousin had told me some things he had done to his wife and some terrible things he had done to the lady he was staying with. Things like pistol whipping her while she was tied to a tree. He said she deserved it because of seeing other men.

I married Lawrence knowing all that I knew and I told him I could deal with everything but the beating. I had been raised once and I wasn't going to take a beating. He did not hit me not once in all the years we were married. He hit beside my head one time when we were married for two years. Jonathan didn't hit me either, but his unfaithfulness hurt worse than a beating. I thought Lawrence wouldn't do this to me because he knew how I felt about it all. I had told him about my first marriage. Lawrence was twelve years older, I thought I could fulfill this man's needs.

We were married February 1, 1969 at my aunt's house on Mockingbird Lane. She and her husband had been living together for four or five years and they got married a few months before December of 1968. A friend of my uncle was a pastor and he married us one Friday night around 8 o'clock.

After we were married, we went out to the club but we didn't stay long. That night we stayed at my aunt's house. Our second night of marriage we stayed at our own place. We planned to get up every Sunday morning and he was going to take me out to my aunts so I could go to church with her. After church we were going grocery shopping, so Lawrence said he was going to ride out for a little while. Lawrence was gone all night until six the next morning. It was our second night. I was so upset I couldn't go to church, but we did get groceries.

I kept my job and I kept working. Lawrence didn't want me to work but I knew I had three children and he also had three. He had a son and two daughters. Lawrence would take me to my aunts for me to go to work and then I would stay with her in the afternoon until he got off. He would pick me up, we'd go home, cook, bathe and go to bed. The weekdays were okay; it was the weekends that weren't. I was determined not to go out with Lawrence anymore. He'd go out and I'd go to church.

We stayed in the apartment for about three months and then we moved into the house next door to my aunt and uncle, which they owned. My uncle, Lawrence's cousin, fixed it up so we could move in it. Before we moved, the owner of the apartments tried to sell it to us but we said no. He told us we could make the house pay for itself because it has three apartments in it. A few years later the interstate was being built and all those homes were bought.

When we moved next door to my aunt she would take me to work and pick me up. I was still working for the state trooper and his wife. They were younger than me. They had a son named Timothy, Tim for short. He really fell in love with me. His wife worked at the bank and was jealous of Tim's feelings for me. She had to bring him to my house on Saturday and Sunday mornings for me to dress him.

They were good people. I worked for them for four years. The wife had decided to stop working and have another baby because her husband had gotten a raise. They helped me get another job with a neighbor about a block away that had three unruly children. The state trooper told me if I had any trouble to let him know.

On my third day of my new job the wife had gone to work, but her husband stayed home. She had a small kitchen and I was in there placing dishes in the dishwasher so I could fix the kid's food when they got up. The husband came into the kitchen with his underclothes on with his arms across the small doorway. I couldn't get by. His oldest child was a seven-year-old girl. I called them to get up and they did. When they got up, he went to the bathroom to get dressed. I told the little girl to wash her face and her two little brothers.

When he came back dressed, I told him he was going to have to stay home and keep his kids because I quit. I called the state trooper and he came and took me home.

I stayed home and kept the house. Lawrence had a good job working for a construction company finishing concrete. We went to T street and furnished our house. We had a living room, two bedrooms and a kitchen. I was so proud of our house. It was the first time in my married life that I had a house with our furniture even though we were renting and the furniture was second hand, it was ours. That summer was the first summer my mom was coming to visit with my three children.

I was so proud. I bought new bedspreads and curtains. I cleaned my house from the front porch to the back door. When my mom got there, she had been with my cousins and uncles. They had been drinking and my mom would drink every now and then, but this time she drank too much. I was showing off my new house and she got sick and vomited right in the middle of my bed. On my new bedspread. I was so hurt and mad at my mom. She not only drank and got sick but she had my children.

I had to strip my bed and wash. I had a washer but no dryer. She kept apologizing over and over again because I was crying.

Two weeks after Emma and my children came, Lawrence's children came from Chicago for the summer. I was pregnant with our first child, Fanita. The summer was great except for one bad experience. Lawrence had bought a car that the brakes did not work when you needed them to. The youngest daughter had gone and stayed with her mom's sister. The two sisters had to have everything alike. The aunt had bought one girl a pair of sandals, but not the other. So, we all loaded up the car.

We rode all over Pensacola trying to find shoes in that size. At one store, a man was working under his car with the jack up. He had just come from under it when Lawrence was trying to stop the car but the brakes would not work. He hit the car and knocked it off the block. But God. We had all the children in the car and no one was hurt and the man didn't press charges. We made it through the 4th of July and everyone returned home safely the last of July.

I didn't work all summer. I really don't know who told Mrs. Eloise about me, but she came to my house one afternoon to ask me to help with her little boy Kip, and her adopted little girl, Liz. I worked for her cleaning after Kip started school and I kept him until she got off work. They were great people. I worked for them approximately three years before her husband's job was transferred. I did not see the husband more than three times. He traveled a lot and he worked long hours. I was up in the morning because then I was making $35.00 a week. I would then send Emma $20.00 a week.

During the summer the girls decided that they wanted to stay with us. The oldest son was already staying with us.

So, we kept them even though the mom wanted them to come back. As a mother I can understand how she felt. We got them ready for school. On the first day of school his son walked the girls to the bus stop which was right down the street. I heard crying and screaming. I was in the house cleaning up and I was six months pregnant.

The oldest girl made it back to the house and grabbed me around the legs and said, "Monk," my nickname also. Her mother was there. Her mom thought she was calling mama. She was cursing and almost pulled me down. I told her I was pregnant but she didn't care, she took them. Right after they left, the son came home with a knife in his hand ready to fight. I thought he was gone too, but he said he wasn't going anywhere. I didn't know who she was but Lawrence's cousin that lived next door to us told me who she was.

Lawrence thinks someone told her the time the children are at the bus stop and the times he is working. One neighbor came out and said I know where Lawrence is working. I will take you there. I went and told Lawrence. He went all over town, airport, bus station, train station and he couldn't find them. He went to his sister in law's house and he beat her. She called the cops but he didn't go to jail. We couldn't get them anymore for the summer for about three years.

Fanita was born on the 5th of December. Emma and my children came back to be with me. We had bottled gas and it would give out in two days. It was a cold, cold night when Fanita was born. Lawrence had stayed with me until after Fanita was born. He left to head home and the car ran out of gas so he had to walk. He said he slept between the mattresses. Lawrence had the gas hooked up on Monday. Everyone was saying how expensive it was but it was the best thing for us that winter.

Fanita was little but cute. My daughter Emma didn't want her because she had gotten used to being the only girl. She told me to give Fanita to my best friend because they didn't have any children. I went back to work for Mrs. Eloise, working five hours. Fanita was almost four months old then. Lawrence's cousin would keep her for me, but they weren't really keeping her clean. There were two old ladies who were retired teachers that asked if they could keep Fanita for me. I said yes. They were great with her.

They potty trained her, taught her how to read and much more. They kept her for about a year. Then the older one began to get sick and the other needed care for her special needs' son. So, I told Mrs. Eloise that I had to quit because I had no one to take care of Fanita.

She said, "bring her with you. Keep her and Liz together." That worked great for a little while but Lawrence didn't approve.

Mrs. Eloise made Liz's clothes and every time she made clothes for Liz she made some for Fanita also. Fanita had beautiful little dresses and shorts sets. I really missed her when they relocated to North Carolina.

I was home only two weeks when the teacher that was keeping Fanita told me about the lady that needed someone to work. She asked if I wanted the job. I said yes. Her name is Mrs. Waters. She was married to a man that dug wells. They were rich. She had a big house on Plantation Road. At that time, it was only her house along those big oak trees. And their lawn was beautiful. She and her husband had divorced and he was staying in a small house on the airport where his business was. Before their divorce she had owned a dress shop in front of her husband's business.

I worked at the dress shop on Tuesday and Thursday and at her house on Monday, Wednesday and Friday. I could get clothes at a discount and put them on layaway also. I bought a few pants sets. Mrs. Waters paid me *$40.00* weekly. I sent *$25.00* and kept *$15.00*.

Guess what happened to her? She sold that land and now its University Mall. But before she did that she kept her grandson for a while because her daughter was having trouble in her marriage. I kept Tim all the way until he was two years old. She sold all her land and moved down with her daughter. Years later after we had moved to Molino she came to show Tim where they used to live. She found out where I lived and brought Tim by to see me. I have not heard from them anymore.

The year was 1971 and Fanita is two years old. I was pregnant this year. I got sick with baby Angela. Emma couldn't come because Tony had just started school. Lawrence's baby sister came to help me get off my feet. I had a daughter named Angela in December of this year. After I had Angela, born prematurely, she was only with me for two days and her little lungs collapsed. She was a beautiful baby.

My marriage was going okay. Lawrence was still going out all night and weekends. He said he was gambling and I believed him. Then I began to hear about all the women he

73

would be with at the clubs and two from the neighborhood. I was really mad at Lawrence and wanted to show him that two can play that game. I had been talking to this guy on the phone, he didn't know about it but Lawrence knew him. Lawrence would've killed us both.

You see, it was okay for him but not me. I met up with the man but I couldn't go through with the affair. One reason was because the man was afraid that Lawrence would find out and he already knew what he would do. I decided I didn't want to break my marriage vows. This is the only time I tried to have an affair even though many men asked me.

# Chapter 5

## ~A new beginning~

Then we started hearing a rumor that Lawrence's cousin, the one married to my aunt, was trying to buy the house we were living in. Lawrence's uncle owned the place and he had promised to sell to us when he got ready to sell because Lawrence had added a room on the back. My aunt told Lawrence that he better find somewhere else to stay because rent was going up and was going to be asking Lawrence to do a lot of fixing up since he was good at it.

Another cousin of Lawrence had heard about them bragging of what they were going to get Lawrence to do. The other cousin came to us one night and told us about a place out in the country where he goes hunting. So, we kept our money and didn't tell my uncle.

In October 1972, I had a little boy. Lawrence was thrilled to have a little boy after having all girls. Lawrence's brother visited us at the time he was born. He is a doctor. He was teasing me that he would deliver the baby. I said no you won't. I named him Marcus Dewon. I gave him the initials M.D because I loved watching Marcus Welby M.D on television. We nicknamed my son BoBo. He was a big healthy baby but he had a lot of allergies. His allergies were so bad he had to go to the doctor at least once a week.

The doctor said it was the atmosphere and if we moved a few miles away he would probably be healed. BoBo wouldn't have anything to do with his daddy. Lawrence wanted to take him with him like he did Fanita. He could take Fanita everywhere with him on Saturday while I went grocery shopping with my aunt. I learned that he didn't mind taking her with him because she was his good luck charm. He had her throwing dice for him when he was gambling.

I found out when she found one in the house. She threw it and said, "7 or 11." I thought he was being nice taking her to buy things at the store while keeping her. All that time she was earning it.

In 1974 I was pregnant again. I didn't work after BoBo was born because he wouldn't let anyone keep him. My cousin had come to stay with me when she finished school. She was the only one that could keep him without him crying. My friend wanted to keep him so bad because she didn't have any children but he wouldn't stay. My cousin that came to stay with me got married on our front porch. She married a young man that we thought she shouldn't marry. They had three boys and were together until he passed away, which was at a young age.

Lawrence's cousin came to us in winter of 1973 and told us about an acre of land and a house for sale for *$5,000.00* in Molino. His cousin had been there hunting with a friend. He told him about a man named Mr. Dewitt needed to sell his house and land because of a divorce. The house was okay. It had been burned a little in two rooms and needed rewiring. The yard was grown up real bad. We talked to Mr. Dewitt and his new wife. She had just come with their new baby.

Mr. Dewitt asked for *$550.00* monthly. In order for us to fix up the house and with me being pregnant we had to borrow the money. We paid them back in two months. We worked on that house and yard all summer long. My cousin who was keeping BoBo said I was working too hard with all the painting and all, but I was so excited. I forgot about the baby. We had planned to move the first week of September and we did. My baby was born in the middle of August.

I was only six months along, they couldn't do anything to keep me from going into labor. He was only with us for four hours. Lawrence named him Jerry. Lawrence blamed me for losing the baby.

Lawrence got the house finished and we were able to move in. Lawrence had told me all about the place and all about the people. He knew some from that area that he had met at different clubs. He talked about the affairs that went on with the other husbands and wives. He was right and I was advised not to associate with them. I took my husband's advice and we moved there in love and totally devoted to each other for three years, or so I thought.

By this time Lawrence was no longer working for the construction company. We had it pretty rough for a year. The phone call back to town was long distance so Lawrence couldn't get connected with people he did work for. The neighbor that lived up the road from us would let us use her phone but we tried not to use it often. They were older people but nice. Everyone in the neighborhood gave them a bad name. They said she practices VooDoo. Everyone was afraid of her, especially my children. She became a friend of mine though.

Fanita started school that year and I didn't have my cousin to take care of her since we had moved to the house in the country. I decided to get my children from my mom so Fanita would have someone to ride the bus with. I went to get them but only Sister and Jr. would come. Tony wanted to stay with Emma but he would come every summer. Then he came to us after he finished school.

Lawrence was working for himself and Mr. Caper part time. He used to work on the side with Mr. Caper when he was at the construction company. After we moved, we didn't have a phone so people couldn't get in touch with Lawrence for jobs. God sent an angel one Sunday morning, it had to be an angel because no one else saw him or knew him. He was a preacher dressed in a three-piece suit, shoes shining and driving a big nice car, I had just finished cooking breakfast and Lawrence was fixing to eat while I got the children up for Sunday school.

Lawrence went to the door to meet him and he was asking Lawrence about different churches. Lawrence didn't know so he invited him in and said, "Virginia do you know this church?" I said no, so we kept naming different ones and he kept saying that's not it.

Lawrence said, "Well, I was about to eat breakfast, would you like some?"

He said, "Yes, I believe I will because those biscuits sure look good."

"I will fix the table and let you eat before I get the children up," I said.

We only had a small table in the kitchen with four chairs. He came and blessed the food after I fixed the table. They ate and he asked a lot of questions. He asked about church. He asked about jobs. The preacher finished eating and said how good the food was.

He started out the door then he turned and told Lawrence, "before time for you to make your payments whatever God lay on your heart, do that."

Remember me telling you about the gambling and card playing. Well, if Lawrence didn't make enough working that week to make the payment, he would try his hand that night. He would win big every time. He would lose if it wasn't payment time. God was making a way. If he won over what we needed he would always help someone.

There was a man that had a little one room house right beside the road. He planted vegetables and sold them. He also sold bait and worms to fishermen. He was a Godsend. He introduced Lawrence to some important people up here. He also showed him how to dig bait and would buy them from him. He let us pick peas or okra on half or all. He rented us a half acre so we could plant beans, peas and he sold them for us. We kept some in the freezer.

He was a great friend in the time of need. When he found out I could sew, he would have me hem his pants. He would find people who need help in their fields and I'd take Jr. and Tony. That's how they bought their first cars. Lawrence told them if they made half the money, he'd give them the other half.

Now Lawrence had gotten us a phone. We still couldn't do a lot of calling because everything was long distance. Lawrence used it for jobs and I would call my aunt once a week and my mom every Friday night. Jobs began to come in from Mr. Caper. He had left his job and went into construction. Lawrence met more people up there in construction. Some worked with Mr. Caper or just helped him from time to time. People up here were always looking for Lawrence once they got to know him.

My children began meeting other children and they told me who everyone was. I stayed busy cooking, cleaning, washing and ironing. I took in a little sewing from ones in the neighborhood. Some were hard to please, but one young lady and her mom I did quite a bit for them.

I got pregnant again with my fifth child for Lawrence. It was 1976. It was a tough pregnancy and I only made it to the seventh month. She was a cute little girl. I named her Kimberly. She was born with her hands up to her chin, like praying hands. She was with us for four days. She had yellow jaundice. The hospital said they did not have the blue light to put her under so we lost her. She looked at us when we went in to touch her. I had a nervous breakdown afterwards.

BoBo tried to take care of me while Lawrence left to go to work. Lawrence would say… "you are the man of the house now, take care of your mom."

The doctor put me on bed rest. BoBo would say, "Lay down, I'll bring you milk." He wanted to give me milk every hour. My mom couldn't come down to care for me because Tony was still in school. The doctor gave me strong medication to help get through the depression.

It was Friday night. Lawrence was still going out on Friday and Saturday night. I took my medicine after the children went to bed and Lawrence went out. I went and laid on the couch and went to sleep. I woke up hours later and I didn't know who or where I was. I walked through the house and didn't know who my children were. The Holy Spirit told me to go back to the couch. When I sat I began to remember.

I thought those were my children! I got up and flushed the medicine down the toilet then fell on my knees and gave thanks to God and asked him to heal me and to help me overcome my depression. I asked for strength to take care of my children no matter what Lawrence was doing or where he'd go.

# Chapter 6

---

## ~The beginning of my work life~

After Kimberly was born and the Lord took her home, I began to get restless with all the children in school. Lawrence was taking care of the bills, but I never had anything for myself and only a little for the children. There was a store and laundromat right up the street. I didn't have a washer or dryer so I would send clothes by Jr. and Sister to wash when Lawrence wouldn't take me. They took one basket full at a time. The owner was Mrs. Higgins.

I would go to the store during the day and out the clothes up. When she would get a new batch of clothes, she would call me. Lawrence didn't want me to work but I decided to find a job anyway. His son came home from the military and he took me to the job service and they sent me to a job. I did housework and sat with a 92-year-old lady, Mrs. Rain. She was great. She lived with her daughters Mrs. Greege and Mrs. Royale. Her husband was a lawyer and deceased. She was battling cancer.

I worked for the agency for three months. Then Mrs. Greege told me to tell the agency that I was quitting, then come back on Monday. I could get all the money that way instead of paying for the agency. I did just that. I finally moved up to *$60.00* a week. I also spent the night on Saturday night to let the sisters go to eat, to a movie or whatever. Mrs. Rain and I stayed home, watched TV and she would tell me about her childhood in Birmingham. She would also tell me if Mrs. Greege was mean to her because Mrs. Royae was kind like her.

She and I would walk around the block every day after her nap and she would talk the whole way. Mrs. Greege decided to sell her house and they moved downtown in the San Carlos Hotel. They had a three bedroom, two-and-a-half-bathroom apartment on the 7th floor. I would take the bus every morning from Ensley and the bus terminal was right in front of the hotel. Before the job ended the bus went all the way north to Century so I could catch the bus much closer to home.

I would run errands for Mrs. Greege, when all the stores were closed. Back then, blacks were not allowed in certain restaurants. Mrs. Greege would send me to those restaurants for desserts once or twice a week. The first time she sent me she told me they aren't going to want to let you in but I am calling over there to tell them they better let you in and not make you wait outside. I will be looking out the window, which looks right down at the restaurant's front door. I went over and opened the door.

The waitress said, "Oh! You know you can't come in here," as she was about to close the door when a man ran over and said, "please let her inside the door. She came for Mrs. Greege."

He told me to wait right there while he got her order. Then he said, "see, Mrs. Greege is looking right at us from her window." He closed the door with me standing right beside it and said don't move. The place was full of people eating dinner. All the forks and knives stopped the whole time I was there. I couldn't help but laugh because I was thinking a few years back I was eating at the table with folks like you. I ate all my meals with the family, they wouldn't let me eat afterwards.

Mrs. Greege was fixing ice tea and she said, "Virginia, do you drink tea?"

I said, "no ma'am."

She said, "well, Virginia what type of person are you? I thought all black people don't drink tea and eat watermelon." Mrs. Greege's mom died and moved out of the state. I didn't hear from them again.

While I was working for Mrs. Greege, on Saturday nights, Lawrence did not stop going out even for one night. He would take the kids to my aunt's house. I would then come home, fix breakfast and get the children ready for Sunday school. Lawrence would be gone all Sunday while we were at church and then he would come home early Sunday evening to rest up for Monday. Things were beginning to get a little rocky between us because Lawrence was beginning to mess around and it was getting back to me.

After Mrs. Greege left, I was out of work and home every day but not for long. I was working in my yard one day when one of the neighbors passed by and asked me if I was working. I told them I was looking for a job. She said that there was a family looking for a nurse's aide. She gave me the name and address. It was the Fillinger's family. I called them and they made an appointment for me to talk with them. They were really nice.

When Lawrence took me over there he said, "you aren't going to be able to work for these people because they were 'Rednecks'."

After the interview they said that they would call me. I said only if it's your will, Lord. The patient's name was Mrs. Fillinger. She was paralyzed from the waist down. I had been trained on how to change beds with patients in them but I hadn't done one by myself.

A week later, I started the job. I fixed her breakfast, gave her a bath, gave medication and washed and folded clothes. Her granddaughter stayed in the house with her. Her granddaughter was married and had three busy body kids. She didn't do anything for herself or her children. If Mrs. Fillinger used the bathroom on herself in the middle of the night it would still be on her when I got there. Mrs. Fillinger was mean and hateful but she was Holy.

She said, "you couldn't wear pants, watch TV, no magazines, no music and no radio."

I would fix her food and she would say how do I know you didn't spit in it, how do I know you are giving me the medicine right? I would go home and pray about how to deal with her. So, I took my bible with me and every time she said something mean, I would ask her to show me it in the bible. She would turn her head to the wall. I did not have one single day off for the first three weeks then I found a girl in the neighborhood who could work some days.

After I had worked for a few weeks I began to see how disturbed she was. She was seeing black dogs with teeth on the wall and I would have to hold her hands to keep her from scraping her face or pulling out her hair. She had long pretty hair that was hard to wash because it tangled easily. I treated her as kindly as possible. She got a bedsore on her butt and I really had to work with her keeping her turned and clean. A nurse from the clinic would come out twice a week to help me with it. The nurse and I got the sore healed. Before the sore got healed it smelled so bad that none of her family members would come into her room to see her.

One day, I went to work and heard her talking but when I went to the door I realized she was praying. She had a "BM" that day and scratched herself and spread it all over her face and hair. I left her alone, didn't clean her up, didn't feed her and I walked out the room. She called me back around 12 o'clock. She prayed for half the day and when I went in she looked like a completely different person. I washed her hair,

89

gave her a bath, changed her bed and fixed her some food. From that day on she did not want me to have a day off and she wouldn't let anyone give her medicine except me.

She began to get better. The sore began to heal. Her children, family and friends began to visit. She would tell everyone about how good I was and that God had sent me to her because she was on her way to hell. She said that she hated black people and used to throw hot water on them when they passed her house. She said she use to bury cats alive and throw boiling water on dogs. She asked for forgiveness when she prayed that day. That's when I learned about, "you reap what you sow."

During the time her friends were coming to visit, there were three people that came to visit and it was, Mr. Henry, Ms. Alex, and Ms. Ella. They has been long time friends of Ms. Fillinger. They saw how well she was doing and had a nice visit. And when they begin to leave, Ms. Ella asked me for my name, address and phone number. She said that they were all getting old and was going to be needing help so she wanted to

keep me in mind. Little did I know that I would end up working for all three of them.

The children began to disagree when she got sick. Some wanted her to go to the hospital while others wanted to grant her wishes of staying home to die. I was there when the ambulance came to take her to the hospital and she began to cry because she didn't want to go. It was out of control. They said before she died that every time a black nurse would enter her room she would say, "Is that you Ginny V?" I did not get to see her before she died. Before she left for the hospital she told her son to get me the best gown and robe set that Vanity Fair sells. He worked at Vanity Fair. It was a beautiful pink set with shoes. I still have it all these years later.

It was 1978, and I was back home again with no job but I was enjoying being home with the kids when they came home from school. I worked at my own pace to do things around the house. It was nice but it didn't last long.

An older lady in the neighborhood worked for some wealthy people and they asked her if she knew anyone that was honest that wanted to work for good people. She came to me and asked me if I was ready to go back to work.

She said, "I know some people that need someone and I think you are the person for them."

I told her that I would give them a try. I could have gotten a job before now but they were all downtown. I did not want the hassle of trying to get back and forth plus, I didn't know how long I would have to leave my children alone. This year I went to work for Mr. and Mrs. Guise. When I went to them I thought they wanted a nurse aide so I showed up in my uniform and name tag. When I got there, we talked and she said that she could do things for herself but she couldn't clean her bathroom, make her bed, vacuum or mop.

She said if you can do it for me I would pay you the same price. I agreed and said I will work today if that is pleasing to you. When I finished they said they were well pleased with my work. They only wanted me one day a week but she said there are a lot of women in my church that need help also. She kept her word and a week later I received a call from Mrs. Henry. It was a small town so everybody knew everybody.

I heard that they never kept anybody and that they didn't pay. They also said that Mr. Henry was prejudiced. I was really nervous because I was going to a Baptist church in the same community. It was a black church and everyone knew him. One lady had worked for him for years and she even bought an acre of land from him. She didn't have anything bad to say except he didn't like to pay so she went to work somewhere else.

My pastor at the time said just because they give him a bad name doesn't mean he is bad. It may be the way they went to him, their attitude or not good work. It was rough at first. Mrs. Henry would lay money all over the place in different rooms. I told her when I started that I didn't steal and that I could get her a reference from my previous jobs. She also had a grandson that was in and out that she was keeping while his mom and dad worked. He was five at the time. I asked her to put the money up because if her grandson got some of the money I did not want to be blamed.

I went back the next week Mr. Henry got some iron frying pans and wanted me to chip off the cake burn grease. I told him I was not going to do that and if he wanted me to do that then I quit.

Mrs. Henry said, "we are sorry and we want you to stay."

I stayed and we became friends as I was with Mrs. Guise. I had two days a week and I wasn't even looking for work. Mr. and Mrs. Guise was God sent. They opened the way for me to do housework in this small town.

Mr. and Mrs. Guise went to the Methodist church and he was a devoted Christian. He followed God's will in every aspect of the word. Mrs. Guise drank wine and played cards the majority of the day. They would have devotion together every morning then they asked me to have it with them when I was there. He taught me about the Holy Spirit. I was going to church every Sunday, teaching the children in Sunday school and listening to the pastor preach.

The pastor where I went to church mainly preached about the bible stories which did not teach you much about the Holy Spirit.

# Chapter 7

## ~Church~

So, I stopped going to the neighborhood church. Let me tell you about my experience there. It was a family church, meaning the church was mainly made up of one family. I went there because it was close and the children and I could walk there. I had been told about how the people behaved but I went and eventually saw for myself. Deacons and others were having affairs within the church. It was bad. I only had a few older women who were friends of mine.

After a few years there, one of the deacon's wives really had it in for me. I was teaching Sunday school and she said I called on everyone but her. I apologized, but she didn't accept it. I ushered and if I was ushering on the side she sits on, she would move to the other side. The pastor asked us into the office and he asked me to apologize again and I did. He asked her if she would accept it and she said she would die and go to hell before she accepted it.

The pastor said that if she didn't accept it he would have to put her out of the church and he did. In the next two weeks every time I arrived for Sunday school they would be having it already and would have already started teaching. I said that was okay with me. I didn't tell you to put her out in the first place.

He said, "you see, this is her family church and they pay my salary."

I kept going then people started telling me that she was carrying a gun for me and if I bump into her she was going to kill me even if it was in church. So, I said okay Lord it is time for me to go, so I did. The week after I left, my daughter and her friend were going up the road and her friend was riding a bike. This woman ran off the road to hit my daughter but hit the girl on the bike instead. And that little girl that grew up in the community. She wasn't hurt badly but did have to go see a doctor. The lady said that she hit the wrong one. We did not get an apology and the pastor was not at that church long before they got rid of him too.

At this time, I was going to another family church in another neighborhood. I wasn't going to church at all but then one day a neighbor pulled her car into our yard and said, "How are you?" She asked my name and she told me hers. We talked for hours. She invited me to come to church with her and her family. I told her I did not drive and she said, "that's okay. My husband has a truck with a camper for the children."

We went to church with them and she became my best friend in this community. She would take me to work. We would go pick beans, peas and cut okra before going to work so we could put them in our freezers for winter because both of our husbands were construction workers and work was slower in the winter months. Back to the church I visited, well, my spiritual mom's oldest daughter was married to the pastor of this church.

It was my first time meeting him. He also pastored the church back home on some Sundays. It was a small world. I remained a member there for *18* years. Everything was great. I taught Sunday school again, ushered and was the treasurer. I even started a willing workers committee.

We were there all those years with a great choir, usher board and youth group. Then one day a lady came to join our church with three small boys calling herself a missionary. Her husband came also, but he did not live long after they joined. Her boys had a little singing group and they did okay but she wanted them at the top of everything in the church. They were bad as all get out.

After her husband passed away, she began to ask me to ride with her to different places. I said okay. When I came back she had told different people that she wasn't going to ride me in the new car she had just bought. I went to her and she said yes, you can't ride in my car. I said okay. Some of the women in the church were starting to believe her. One day it got so bad that my girls wanted to fight her. I said oh no! We will not be doing that. I remember my grandfather telling us about a fight being in the church.

The man that was fighting had a stroke when he hit the other man. I prayed about it and was led to scripture, Matthew 10:14. I talked to the pastor and he called a meeting. She told everyone that he was on my side because he was married to my cousin and she wasn't listening to anything he had to say. I left Sunday alone, with my children and two or three other families. We didn't know the pastor was leaving because he stayed and preached, but he left also. Three weeks later when the missionary had broken up the church she left also.

# Chapter 8

---

## ~Work life~

My work life has continued on through all of this. I was still working for the Guise family on Mondays and the Henry's on Wednesdays. Mr. Guise was retired from the Navy so he would go shopping on the Navy base and he would always include canned goods for us. Mr. Henry was a retired saw mill worker and his wife was a teacher. After I was with them for a while Mrs. Henry sister in law, Ms. Alex asked me to work for her on Tuesdays. And he furnished my transportation.

Mr. Guise would pick me up and bring me home. Another great thing about it was I would only work 9 to 2 so I would be home when the kids made it from school. My older children got home later than my son BoBo, so I would always try to make it there before he got off the bus. If I was late I knew the bus driver and she would keep him with her until she stopped the other kids off then she'd bring him back. She was the bus driver for all of my children and a few of my grands before she retired. She was great.

Work was booming for me. Two days opened up for me to work for Mrs. Henry's daughter, Mr. and Mrs. Carols who owned a campground. They rented out spaces to campers, had a swimming hole and fishing ponds. This family lived in a double wide trailer on the campground. So now I have four days a week. BoBo was now in school by this time so it allowed me to work longer. Mr. Carols would provide my transportation. Carols day was Friday.

A few weeks later, a lady came to the Henry's house and asked if she knew me because she had heard that I was working for her. Mrs. Henry said she is here now and she introduced us. She introduced me to Mrs. M. Scottsdale. Mrs. Scottsdale wanted me to work for her mother, who had a trailer right outside of their house. She was a really nice person. I worked for her mother and it wasn't long before she fell and broke her hip. After that she went into a nursing home. Then I started working for Mrs. Scottsdale and her husband. He would take me home after I worked also.

While I was working Mr. Henry and the Scottsdales, I begin to have backaches, so I went to the doctor and then I found out I was pregnant with my ninth child. I couldn't work too much because I had trouble carrying my baby full term.

My oldest daughter finishing school so I let her work one day for Mrs. Henry and Mrs. Scottsdale in order to have money for the summer until I was able to work again. She kept my jobs open til I was able to go back to work.

At that time Sheena, was born. I stayed off work for two months. Then, when I went back to work, I began to also work for Mr. Henry's sister, Ms. Alex. She was never married. She retired from the paper plant. I worked for her three hours and I went to her house after I went to Mr. and Mrs. Henry. I went to them from 9 to 2 and for her 2 to 5. I also worked for Mr. and Mrs. Carols, which gave me five working days.

When I was working for Mrs. Henry, when I got to work in the morning we would talk about thirty-minutes before work about the family, work or whatever. I also did the same thing with the Guise. We would have morning devotions when I first arrived at their house in the morning. And Mr. Guise would go to his study and read the bible.

One day when I went there from work she had been to church that Sunday and she told me, "Virginia, I am not playing cards anymore. I'm not drinking wine anymore. I went to church and a visiting lady was there and she sang *'He Touched Me'* and after that song - He really did touch me. And now I am a different person." She bought a little plaque with "He Touched Me" on it and kept it until just before she died, then she gave it to me. I still have it.

Then while working for the Guise, Mrs. Guise passed away and Mr. and Mrs. Henry asked me if I wanted to go to the funeral with them. While we were on our way back from her funeral, Mrs. Henry asked me if she died would I continue to work for Mr. Henry as I was going to be working for Mr. Guise. I told her I don't know because I didn't know if he would want me to continue working for him.

While working with Ms. Henry in the morning that I would work for her she would go out and fish. They had a fishing pond. She would stay out there all morning because she loved to fish. Then her daughter, Mrs. Carols had a baby. After she went back to work Ms. Henry would keep her baby. I would see to the baby while Mrs. Henry fished. Mr. Henry stayed busy out there doing something all the time or going places.

I would wash, clean but she did all the cooking. She would fix three meals a day. They ate the largest meal in the middle of the day. And she would have to fix a full course meal including dessert because that is what Mr. Henry wanted.

She would always invite Mr. Carols; and kept the campground until he began working full time for the school board. He played the organ for a Methodist church.

Mr. and Mrs. Henry always celebrate Christmas in a big way, with a large tree. He would never use a cedar tree; he always used long needled pine trees which were beautiful. The tree was put up in the living room near the fireplace. I would be the one to decorate the tree and take down the decorations after the holiday, which I enjoyed doing.

During the next spring, Mrs. Henry began to not feel like fishing, not wanting to go shopping and was asking me to see the baby more than what she had been. I began to tell Ms. Carol and Mr. Henry, that I believed that she was sick or not feeling well but they wouldn't listen. They would say she just needed rest. She got sick and had to go to the doctor and from the doctor to the hospital. They called in her family and she passed away.

Remember me saying how she wanted me to work for her husband on our way from Ms. Guise funeral, well now is the time. We will see. After she died, I went to work that morning and he was so pleasant, so not the same Mr. Henry. I was so nervous, because we have not ever sat and talked. But he said, "Virginia, come in and sit and talk with me like you did with Mrs. Henry."

He told me how pleased he was with my work. Showed how he liked his towels and clothes folded and how he liked the sheets on the bed. He told me how he liked his clothes and underclothes placed in the drawer, always with the clean ones at the bottom. After Mrs. Henry died, he stayed a widow for about three years. Then he met Ms. Katie. He brought her to meet me and said they were getting married soon.

I said, "Okay, she can let me know what she wants me to do when she gets here."

And Mr. Henry said, "Oh no, you're going to do everything just like you've been doing because you know how I like it done."

I did that for the thirteen years that they were married. I also went to Ms. Katie to clean for her from time to time because they kept both houses. They would stay at his house from Sunday to Wednesday.

While I was still working with Mr. Henry, I was also working for the Scottsdale, Ms. Alex and the Carols. Then I began to work for Ms. Ella which was Mr. Henry and Ms. Alex's oldest sister. Remember when I said the three friends that visited Ms. Fillinger, well here we are, they are the three. Ms. Alex had to leave her house and move in with her sister, Holly because they did not want her to stay in the house by herself after she had pneumonia.

Ms. Alex has a bedroom, a bath and a sitting room at her sister's house. I continued to work for her and did light house work for her sister. About two years later, her sister Holly was diagnosed with a brain tumor. So, Ms. Alex had to move in with her oldest sister, Ms. Ella. She had her own bedroom and bathroom downstairs. And Ms. Ella had her own bed and bath upstairs. She was the only member of the Henry family that was not Methodist.

She was Pentecostal holiness, just like her friend, Ms. Fillinger, but totally different. She wore pants to do yard work but they couldn't have a zipper in the front. She was devoted to her church and went every Sunday; to Sunday school and church. She drove herself even in her 90's. I went to church a few times and she had me teach Sunday school. I was a little nervous because I am Baptist. But God.

She always remembered me and Lawrence on our anniversary and would give me something from her kitchen, like crystal. She said her children and grands already had enough. She told me when I first started working with her she was going to walk upstairs every day and the day that you come to work and she wasn't downstairs, that was the day she was going to die. Because she was always up fixing breakfast for her and Ms. Alex. She cooked three meals a day, worked in the yard, drove herself to appointments and to her daughter and son.

She also took me to work for her daughter a few times because her daughter had to take in two of her grandchildren for a while. Her oldest son's wife had cancer and I also worked for them once a week. Her daughter in law was the daughter of her friend, Ms. Fillinger. The daughter did not live long. About a year and half later I came to work and she was upstairs. I asked Ms. Alex where was Ms. Ella. I was thinking she was outside some place.

Ms. Alex said, "she did not come down this morning and you remember what she said?"

I said, "I remember." Then I called her and went upstairs. She was in bed.

She said, "fix Ms. Alex some breakfast, then come back." I did. When I went upstairs, Ms. Ella asked me to take her hand and pray for her. I was like, me, pray for you? She said yes, you can do it. I took her hand and began to pray.

After prayer, she said, "call my daughter and tell her to come and fix me some stewed beef." I called her daughter and she said, "I'm not coming up there, I have things to do."

I said, "but your mom is in bed."

She said, "good. She needs to rest." I told Ms. Ella what she said. Ms. Ella said ok.

She then said, "tell Mr. Henry to come over."

I went to Mr. Henry's house and he said he was busy, what does she want?

I said, "she's in bed."

He said, "good. She needs to rest."

I went back and told her what he said. I helped Ms. Alex get dress. Then Ms. Ella called and said for me to call the ambulance, I thought I wanted to die at home but maybe I shouldn't. I called the ambulance.

Then here come Mr. Henry, he asked, "what's going on?"

I said, "she sent for you, but you did not come." They started out the door but she died just before they left the house. She said, "God Bless you and take care of Ms. Alex."

I called her daughter and she began to cry and said she was coming because she did not want me to take anything. I said I only was going to take care of Ms. Alex. Then Mrs. Carol came home from school. I called her daughter in law, the wife of her youngest son, who was her power of attorney. He was out of the country. He told me not to let his sister move anything. His wife came before his sister. She was the first one to leave me something in her will.

In '83, I was still working for the Scottsdales, then I got pregnant with my last child. I did not work for her until two months after my baby was born. This time my oldest daughter had her own job so she couldn't work for me. At this time, I was also working for Mrs. Carol, Ms. Alex and the 2nd Mrs. Guise. Ms. Scottsdale was not working full time anymore. She was a substitute teacher. She would go with me to school for children for parent's day. She would let them pick up pecans on their property and keep them. The kids would sell them for money to go to the fair.

One day when I was working for her, Mr. and Mrs. North came by. They were moving to Molino from Scenic Hills.

I had a full week and I kept it up for quite some time. Mrs. North asked me if I would work for her. I had some afternoons available so I worked for Mr. and Mrs. North. So, I would leave the Scottsdale's house and go to the North's house to clean. The North's were great people, but they loved their alcohol. They had one child who had gotten killed while he was in college. They drank away their pain. Mrs. North loved the movie *'Gone With the Wind'* and she would call me her "mammie."

After watching the movie, I felt it was an honor. Mrs. North got sick and while her sister came to visit she told her what she wanted me to have. It was a television, a set of china and two chairs from her living room. Her sister also gave me a cup set and faces with heads that looked like famous people. I had 12. When I went to the antique store I realized that they were worth more than I imagined.

I worked for these people for years. They were not only my employers but they were also my friends. Years later I still am in contact with some of the family members of the people I worked for. Years went by. Life happened.

And along the way you learn some things. People may not always be fair but that is not my responsibility. My responsibility is to give my best.

During this time, the second Mrs. Guise was moving back to her home in Tennessee after Mr. Guise died. The man from the church that was helping her move said his wife needed someone to work for them because his wife had lupus. I said ok and I went to meet them. She was awesome. I worked for them until 2007 when the stock market went bottom up. Mr. Claude said he did not want me to work for them anymore. I tried to convince him to let me do less hours for less money so that I could keep the dust down because Ms. Claude only had one lung. I had to stop. I did not work for them anymore.

8 years later, Ms. Claude told me about her cousin when I saw her at her stop. Her name is Ms. Mason. Ms. Mason had cancer and couldn't walk but she could do things with her hands like fold clothes. She was unable to sweep, mop or vacuum. Her husband never did any house work so he was lost. He was so patient and loving towards her. I thought I was there for her in the beginning, but I believe the Lord had me there for her husband instead.

He was broken up over her not being able to do anything. Then found out that the doctors could not do anything for her anymore. He called her his Proverb 31 wife. She did everything until she couldn't, for family and friends. He tried hard but couldn't because he never had to before. She would get upset with him. So, I would have to talk to her and calm her down. He would take me home. So, one day he confided in me about not having insurance and he was selling and doing all he could so he could give her a good funeral.

This is the hard part, knowing that he was raising the money for himself. He died of a heartache two months before she did. She was with him alone when he died. She never got over the experience she had with him. Her sister came in and worked with her. Ms. Mason had two sons. She did not want hospice but we talked her into it. I also told her that I had hospice with my husband. She said ok as long as you are going to be there. After her sisters came I did not go anymore for a while because one son moved in with her. She sent for me and I went to see her. She said she loved me and that she appreciates everything that I had done for her and her husband. She died less than a week later. They were a devoted couple to each other, family and friends.

After the Masons died, two years later Ms. Claude died. So, after Ms. Claude died, her sons and friends from the historical society asked me would I work for Mr. Claude again. I really didn't want to, especially after I went back to the house. She hadn't had anyone in the house to clean for her in the ten years since I left. I was so angry until I started not to work for him. I prayed about it and I know that was something that she would have wanted me to do. So, guess what? I'm still here.

Fast forward to the Christmas of 2009. We celebrate Christ's birthday. No one is at home now but me and Lawrence. All the children are out of the house and there are no sounds of my grandchildren's feet running across the floor. After 40 years of marriage the house was quiet. It was a beautiful day, only a little cool and cloudy. There was a thunderstorm last night with tornado watches all around us. But God protected us.

I cooked collard greens, cabbage, macaroni and cheese, dressing, cornbread, fried chicken, turkey, ham and two sweet potato pies. We were expecting the family to come over later. Right before Christmas, Lawrence had two appointments and Fanita and I both went. During this time, I was working for

Mr. and Mrs. Shell and they gave me the day off so I could go to the doctor with Lawrence. They gave me a paid day off plus a *$50.00-dollar* gift. We went to the eye doctor first and he could read better because earlier in the year he had cataracts removed from his eyes.

But then he began to have headaches and the doctor said that if they did not go away, he might have to have surgery. We left that appointment and went to the lung specialist. Lawrence had a CAT scan two weeks before and the doctor wanted to talk to him about the results. The doctor said that there was a spot on the left lung and it's larger than it was in August. So, they set him up for a biopsy. Much was going through our heads on Christmas day.

I always met with my family before Christmas so they could spend Christmas with their family or visit their in-laws. I received some great gifts this year including a cell phone, shoes, purse and much needed money. Lawrence got money and clothes. And that is how we spent Christmas, spending time with some family and thinking of others.

Lawrence's eye doctor concluded that he needed to have the surgery. He also passed the test to determine if he could have the surgery or radiation for the spot found on his lung. It seemed like it took forever for the lung specialist to get in contact with us about the results of the biopsy. So, after a few days, we called them and they told us to come in. Fanita took us. The doctor said the spot was cancer and that Lawrence did not qualify for surgery or chemo because of everything else going on in his body.

Remember Lawrence used to love going out, drinking, smoking and he had begun to have trouble breathing. All the trouble breathing wasn't from the spot on his lung but from all the years of smoking. The doctor wanted Lawrence to have radiation for six weeks. Fanita and Jr. took him every day for six weeks. I was still working and God made a way for Lawrence and I to get to where we needed to be. Fanita helped Lawrence and my friend, Val helped me.

Lawrence then had a bone scan and fortunately it only showed him having Arthritis. I am at a new church now and the pastor have joined me in praying to help Lawrence see. The church gave us money to help out with some of our expenses. Some of Lawrence's family visited and brought food and money. Blessings were coming from many directions. Remember how I said how Lawrence did for his family? Well, he had three nieces that threw him a surprise party. He went because he thought it was a party for his sister which was a few days before his. When we got there, there were so many nieces, nephews, sisters and brothers from both families. They gave him almost *$1,000* dollars that day.

Our house was needing work badly and I was trying to work out a way to save money to get it done. I was responsible for all the bills now. He did help with the electric bill, car responsibility and medication. I did not know where the money was going to come from, but Good has never failed me. Lawrence got a check from one of his accidents from years ago. He gave me what we needed to fix the house up. I got my grandsons to help me paint the living room, kitchen and hallway. I was even able to buy a new rug for the living room and new material to cover the couch pillows.

It's been almost a year since we heard the results from the doctor. We went to the doctor in September and we found out the cancer has gotten worse. Lawrence was beginning to talk to me in a hateful way. I knew he was sick but it was hard for me to keep my mouth closed and pray daily for a good attitude. I was learning to do it but it wasn't easy. Lawrence went to the cancer center to see a specialist and he prescribed medication for him to take. Later that month he was getting weak in the body. I had to help him out of the tub because he wouldn't let me call my son in law to help us. We got the new medication, it had many side effects but the doctor said it made cancer smaller.

It is now May, 2011 and Lawrence has been off of the cancer medication for almost three months now. Lawrence began to act very differently. He said things like he was going to kill me and that I was acting like his first wife. I would get scared because he would carry a gun in his pocket, under the pillow at night and under the couch during the day. Anytime someone would come, he would grab the gun.

I went and stayed with my youngest daughter, Sheena. He was calling me to come back because no one was coming to see him and no one was cooking his food. I prayed about it and the Holy Spirit spoke to me, have no fear. I am with you always. I went back home determined not to let fear drive me out of my own home. We went to the doctor thinking that all of these changes were side effects of the medication. Wrong, he was accusing me of having an affair. I couldn't seem to do anything right.

He decided to go to church but didn't want to go to the church I attended. I asked him where he wanted to go and I named some churches and the pastors. He said he wanted to go hear Rev. Johnson. He had been going for four Sundays and Lawrence told me that he is not interested in joining a church. He also bought a bible but hasn't stopped talking mean. He wanted to go to another church so we went to a church where some of the children go.

I had been there before and I loved the way they greeted everyone with a hug. The pastor is young but he preaches from the bible. After church Lawrence wanted to go to Barnhill, but didn't want to go because I did not like riding with him too far from home.

We went home and I went to take a nap. He was waiting for me to wake up and he said that we were not moving forward. He said that we did not talk or do things together and he said I had a bad attitude. I told him unless Jesus saves his life then we wouldn't be on the same page.

It is December and I am waiting to go to Texas for my grandson's graduation from the Air Force. I had been planning this trip since before Thanksgiving and was not sure if I was going to be able to make it. The week before Christmas the bottom fell out. I had so many bills to pay and so much to take care of for the house and Lawrence. Instead of putting my trust in God I had put it in the people I was working for. But God showed me that I was putting my trust in the wrong one.

God taught me to trust him. The days I didn't work the people paid me anyways and one of them gave me a bonus. Everything came right on time. Everything worked out. What a God we serve. We headed to the base. We relaxed and enjoyed each other after the celebration. It was great to get away and just spend time with my family. We walked the nature trail and went to a parade.

As time went on Lawrence passed, but I had my family around me. The month after he died, my oldest son and his wife's family were going to the mountains in Tennessee. They invited me to go. I did not want to go but everyone thought it was a good idea for me to get away. When I got away, it was awesome. We went to a shopping center in Gatlinburg and I bought gifts for kids, the grands and even great grands. On the other days I stayed at the house and enjoyed sitting on the porch in the big rocking chairs overlooking the valley. I would sit and write in my book. Oh, it was so relaxing and gave me the time to think where to go from here. But God was with me every step of the way.

I thank God for all the years of marriage and for the people he put in my life. My son in law was put in my life for such a time as this. I would be like oh! How did you know I wanted this? He would say, "I remember hearing you say it over the years." He and my daughter helped me do my house beautifully. He did my guest room in November 2012. I put my mom's bed in it that my dad had bought in 1944. My oldest son helped when he could, he put in windows and other things. I rented a dumpster because we had so much stuff accumulated ever since moving here in 1974. I gave Lawrence clothes to his sons, brothers and grands as well as his hats.

Little by little we sold some of Lawrence's things. Like his old truck and some scrap iron. With that money I fixed up the house. I had everything I dreamed of. Lawrence said our home should be for anyone that needed a place to stay. And that has definitely been the case

My grandchildren were growing up. I am going to be a great grandmother again. And another granddaughter is engaged. And my baby girl called and told me she was going to reenlist for another six years. She also got a promotion. 2012 is bringing change.

I love lighthouses and I was blessed to be taken to see the lighthouse in Pensacola by two of my granddaughters, the two that were brought up in my house. We went up to the top and that was so awesome.

And another thing happened to me with one of my granddaughters. I loved to listen to Joyce Myers and she took me and my 2nd oldest daughter to see Joyce Myers.

# Chapter 8

---

## ~Working years~

I was still working for Mr. and Mrs. Henry, Guises, Carols and Alex; then I got a job with Mr. and Mrs. Ray through Lawrence. He was a teacher at the school where my children were going and she was a secretary at the hospital. She was really nice, but he was always telling on Fanita. She was in his history class. I got pregnant with my 9th child. It was 1981 the year my daughter Sheena was born. Mr. Ray thought my baby was white because she was light skinned. Mrs. Ray told him most all black babies are born that way. He thought that they were all born darker. After school that year they moved back to their small town in Alabama.

Lawrence did concrete for Mr. Watson and he asked Lawrence if he knew of anyone that did housework. He told him that I did housework and that I was the best. I started working for them the following Tuesday. Every time I got out of work someone was waiting to fill the other family's spot.

My oldest son was out of school and could not find work. He quit school at sixteen and he was too young for Lawrence to take him to work with him so he kept Sheena and took me back and forth to work. They were so glad when Sheena was born because there was a baby around. BoBo was now nine and little Kim did not live. Sheena was spoiled rotten.

This worked well for a couple of years. Guess what? I was pregnant again with my 10th child. By this time my oldest daughter was out of high school. That summer she worked for Mrs. Scottsdale and Mrs. Henry one day a week until my baby Regina, was born. Then I went back to work.

At this time Ms. Alex had pneumonia and could not stay by herself anymore so she moved in with her sister. I started working for her half a day and the Henrys the other half of the day. Their yards were connected so I could walk.

While Ms. Alex was with her sister. She added a bedroom, bath and sitting room to her house. I also did light housework for her sister. Ms. Alex was there two years when her sister was diagnosed with a tumor. So, Ms. Alex had to move again, this time she moved in with her oldest sister.

Ms. Alex stayed down stairs and her sister stayed upstairs. I worked for Ms. Alex's sister as well.

These three I met when I was working for Mrs. Fillinger. At this point I had been working for Mr. and Mrs. Henry and Ms. Alex since 1976. Ms. Alex was awesome. She kept a small drawer full of cards and gifts to give out for birthdays and other special occasions. She was the first person I worked for that remembered all my children's names and birthdays. She even kept up with their grades.

Ms. Alex's oldest sister was the only one who was not Methodist. She was Pentecostal Holiness just like her friend I had worked for but she was totally different. She wore pants to do yard work and even when it was cold. She was devoted to her church. She drove herself even at the age of 90. I went to church with her a few times and she asked me to teach Sunday school.

The Carols, who were Henry's children, lived in the country and rented a campground. She was a teacher at the local middle school and he worked at the campground and well as with the fire department. In 1985 she had a daughter born in between my girls and what a blessing that was. BoBo got the hand me downs from her son and the girls got some from her daughter. Her husband passed away in 1986. She had so much support from her parents. They kept her daughter while she worked. Her sister came and stayed with her while she got everything taken care of.

I worked for Mrs. Carol for many reasons but one was because she would not always feel well. She sometimes had migraines, headaches and heart problems. She and I didn't always get along. We got into a huge argument one Christmas. For Christmas, someone had given her daughter two gold chain necklaces. After Christmas, I come back to work and Mrs. Carol asked me if I saw the necklaces. I told her yes and that I thought they were beautiful.

Mrs. Carol said, "I am missing one and I know you have two girls, did you take one?" I laughed.

Then I told Mrs. Carol, "you know I don't steal and why would I give one of my girls a gold chain and not the other? I would also have a hard time explaining gold necklaces to my husband and other children." I finished working that day. A few days later, Mrs. Carol called to say she was sorry and that she found the necklace. I was hurt because I had worked for her for nine years at this point.

Mrs. Henry kept her granddaughter and she would go fishing while the little girl took a nap. I would watch out for her; Mrs. Henry asked me to please keep working for Mrs. Carol. She said her granddaughter was learning to wash and iron. I said, "I can't promise you that because she was only five years old." I might not be working for Carol later.

In 1987, Mrs. Guise passed away and I went to her funeral with Mr. and Mrs. Henry. Mrs. Guise asked me if I would still work for her husband and I told her yes. Mrs. Henry asked me the same thing on the way home. I said I don't know because he may not want me to. I could tell her health was declining. She started to fish less and began to take more naps. I told Mr. Henry and he would just say that she needed rest. I told Mrs. Carol and she said the same thing.

Mrs. Henry would continue to cook large meals in the middle of the day and she began to ask me for help. Soon after, she had a heart attack in 1988 and passed away. Mr. Henry's daughter came home and she asked me to work for him.

I was still work for Mr. Guise but he was going back and forth to visit his sister in Tennessee. I would get the mail and make sure everything was dusted before he came home. One of his neighbors moved back. They used to visit every month to go to the Navy base, visit doctors and shop. When they visited they would bring food and gifts. When they came back they asked me if I would come work for them. I said yes!

Mr. and Mrs. Bradley moved in. He was a retired preacher and she was a housewife. She had cancer. Mr. Guise asked me if I would help them, so I did. She was a remarkable woman. After I worked for them a while I said she should have been a preacher. She did much of the cooking and washing for as long as she could. I told her I did not mind washing the clothes. Then Mr. Bradley began to do the cooking or he got take out. Hospice soon had to come in and they brought a bed. She said I am not going to get in that bed until the day I die. She wrote out her funeral program and all.

I went in one day and she said Virginia, make the hospice bed. I made up the bed, helped her get a shower, she got in it and said to call the nurse. I called the nurse and he began to cry. I talked to him and told him to go play with his goats. So, he went outside. Before she died she told me that she wouldn't be surprised if Mr. Bradley married on the way back from the funeral. He almost did. I worked for him for three more months and then he had a lady friend over. His children had a fit.

His children took out their mom's things then Mr. Bradley sold the house. He moved to Alabama. He also sent me a very sweet letter but I did not see him anymore. Two or three years later, I heard that he got sick and his new wife brought him to his daughter.

Mr. Guise was a widower for one year, during that time he made trips to visit his sister. He met a friend of his sister's and in a few months, they were married. He told me that I could still work for him because his new wife wanted me too. She was younger, outgoing and didn't say much. They were married for six years. Five of those years were great then he began to battle dementia. He had a study and he would go in and read his bible. The first thing his wife did was stop him from studying and she changed that room into a bedroom.

Then she took the car keys so that he couldn't drive. He really didn't like that. He began to call her by his first wife's name; his wife would get mad. He always remembered me and would ask me where his wife was and who was this woman? I would try to explain but he did not understand. One day he told me he knew about a book he could not remember the name of. I told him it was the bible and that he read it every day.

He said, "I don't remember."

I said, "It's Okay. It's in your heart."

He said, "Yes, Yes."

My mom was sick with breast cancer, so I had to go see her on weekends and for doctor's appointments. I told Mrs. Guise I was going to have to be off in order to go see my mom. She told me no because her children were supposed to be coming that weekend. I told her the beds were clean and that her children are younger than I am. She said well you can stay gone. I said fine with me. Mr. Guise told me to do what I needed to do. I did not go back to her when I came back the following week.

The next week they came over to the house, she begged me to come back because he had been asking for me. I told her I would come back to work but if he passed away before her I would be finished.

She began to be extra kind to me. He passed away a few months later. She asked me to continue to work for her. She said she would continue to pay me the same. She stayed a year and then decided to move back home close to her children. A man from church came to help pack up her things. He was Mr. Claude, he said his wife needed help because she couldn't stand dust, she has lupus and only had one Kidney. I told him I would talk to her and we will see.

I did and started with her a week after Mrs. Guise left. Mrs. Guise wrote me a Christmas letter every year. She died a few years later. Her daughter called and told me that I was in her will. I thought it was the items that Mr. Guise left me but it wasn't.

The Claudes' were nice. When Lawrence took me there he said, "Oh, I know them, they are nice people." He poured the concrete for his barn and driveway. They were almost Methodist. Mr. Claude would pick me up and Mrs. Claude would bring me home. I would talk to her and she would give me advice about my marriage. I enjoyed working for them. In 2007 when the stock market crashed, he said that he could not use me anymore. I tried everything, offering less money, cutting my hours back but he still said no. I was doing it for her because I knew God was going to make a way for me.

During this time working for the Scottsdales, on Thursday. She was a teacher and her husband were retired from a plant. She had begun to substitute teach, so I only worked for her *9* to *1*. Friends of the Scottsdales stopped by and they had built a house in a small town. They were neighbors to the Scottsdale's sister. They wanted someone to work for them.

Mrs. Scottsdale said, "maybe you can work for them when you leave my house; they shouldn't need anyone for more than three or four hours.

Mr. and Mrs. North moved into their house within two weeks. Mrs. Scottsdale took me over to their house. They were good people but they were fond of alcohol. They had one child that passed away in college. They never got over the death of their son.

After I had been working for them for two years they began to drink more and eat less. On my birthday they gave me a party at my house. They were getting ready to bring me home with cake, wine and some stronger liquor for them and Lawrence. The phone rang and Fanita had an accident. Fanita was not hurt but the car was wrecked. Lawrence went with Nita to the hospital. Sheena was working after school at the boy's ranch. I asked them to take me to get Sheena and they did. They teased Sheena because she had paint all over her. They were also proud of her work

Mrs. North began to get sick. When I got to work the bathroom and sometimes the bedroom would be messed up.

Sometimes I would encourage her to eat a little something. Mr. North was still driving and taking care of business. Mrs. North then got where she would only stay on the couch because she was close by the bathroom in the hallway. I had to help her to the bathroom. I told her she should tell her sister how sick she was. She said no because she did not want them to know.

I asked Mr. North, was he going to tell her sisters and he said no because his wife didn't want him to. One day her sister called and I answered the phone. Mr. North wasn't there and Mrs. North was sleeping. I told her sister about her and she said she was coming. I told her to tell Mrs. North that she was just coming to visit and not to mention that I had spoken to her. Mrs. North's sister came the following week and saw the shape she was in. At this point in time I was going two afternoons a week.

Her sister stayed two weeks. Mrs. North told her how much she loved me and wanted me to have anything I asked for in the house. She had to tell the sister so I would have a witness.

I was working for Mrs. Mary two days a week on Mondays and Fridays. When I came home on Friday evening Lawrence told me that Mrs. North had called and wanted me to come over. I was like, "Oh Lord, what's wrong?" I called her back and she said that she had been calling Mr. North but that he was not answering and didn't help her to the bathroom. Lawrence took me. They didn't live far from us.

When I got there she was sitting on the couch in a mess. She had not been to the bathroom since I left the day before. She said please clean me up then look for Clint. I got her up, put her in the tub of warm water and cleaned her up. I tried calling Mr. North but he did not answer. I began to run from room to room. I went to their bedroom. I went to their bathroom. He was on the floor, no clothes on but still alive. Thank God.

I went and told her, she said call my neighbor and they will come and help. They would not answer the phone either. I knew they were home because all the lights were on and both cars were in the driveway. I got her out of the tub and back on the couch after I thoroughly cleaned it. She was disappointed that the neighbors did not answer because they had loved and did so much for their little boy. I needed help so I called another neighbor and they came right on over.

We got him into some pajamas and into bed. She said let's call the ambulance. The life flight came. All the neighbors came to see what happened except for the ones next door that I called for help. The paramedics said that Mr. North had to go to the hospital. The last words I heard him say is Virginia, take care of Momma, Mrs. North. The next day I went to my day job and Fanita came to stay with Mrs. North. I would stay at night.

The next day I took off work so that me and a neighbor could take Mrs. North to the hospital. They let me go in with her to see him. The doctor told her that Mr. North did not have long to live, maybe two days. When we got back to the house she begged me not to leave her.

During this time Mrs. North's sister did not come. Mr. North had a brother that he didn't get along with who lived in Alabama and he had a sister that was out of the country. Mrs. North told me to get her dressed and she was going to see her attorney. The attorney was a friend of the family and he had come to pick her up. On her way out the door she had got the call that Clint passed. So, she rescheduled the appointment.

The North's attorney and friend knew Lawrence because he had done concrete work for him in the past. He told me that he was going to pay me and Fanita when this is over because the family is coming in now and they might not believe you. Sure enough Mr. North's brother came first, then her sister. Two weeks later Mrs. North passed away.

Mr. North had a black friend that he worked with also. He was a preacher. Mr. North said he wanted his friend to preach at their funeral. Mr. North just wanted a graveside service. He told his friend not to be scared because he had already hired bodyguards. The only black people there were the preacher and his wife, Fanita, her husband and me. Oftentimes, the preacher shakes the family hand at the end of the funeral. His sister, his brother, neither his mom would shake the preacher's hand. Everything was repeated at her funeral.

Sometimes God can send a blessing your way and fear can cause you not to receive it. On the last day, Mr. North took me home, he said, "Virginia, I know you are not going to let me give you money, but will you borrow any amount you like and you don't have to pay it back. No one knows but you and me. I said no because I did not want to be in debt to anyone and I didn't want to have to try to explain to my husband where the money came from. When his brother came he said they had found over $3,000.00 in the truck.

I said to myself, "Wow, that's what he was trying to give me." Later on, his friend came over and paid me and Fanita the hours we worked. That ended my time with the Norths.

I was still working for Henrys, Alexs', Carols', and Scottsdales. Mrs. Henry had a friend that came to fish with her, Mrs. McCord. Mrs. McCord was a retired teacher also and her husband was a retired preacher. They bought some land from the Henrys and built a house on a beautiful hill overlooking the lake. They were planning on fishing every Wednesday. Mrs. Henry asked me if I would work for them after they finished their house. I did but not before Mrs. Henry died.

When I worked for the McCords, their house was not bad, just dusty with cobwebs everywhere. I didn't mind them in the main part of the house. They had a beautiful screened porch with sliding doors from the living and dining area. The porch was covered with cobwebs and big spiders. He asked me to clean it. I told him no.

I said, "I am not going out there. If you tell your son to clean it out then I will clean it."

He said, "I thought you were supposed to do what I tell you to?"

I said, "I am not doing that so I guess I won't be coming back." I guess Mrs. McCord must have talked to him because before I left that day he said he was sorry and did not know because they had never had anyone work for them. We became friends.

Mr. McCord was a diabetic. He was taking insulin but he did not want to eat right or exercise. I told him I know he could be disciplined because he was a child of God. He started doing better for a little while but then he fell while Mrs. McCord was alone with him. She had to call the ambulance. He didn't break any bones but he was shaky from his blood sugar being high. Caring for Mr. McCord was taking toll on Ms. McCord so she asked me to work two days a week. So, I did.

Later on, their children talked them into assisted living. They moved into an assisted living facility just north of where they lived. It was really nice. Mr. McCord said I missed my calling. He said I should have been a nurse or evangelist. When we were talking I found out that he was the pastor of a church in my hometown. I was shocked.

When they left, they gave me blueberry bushes because I said I wanted one. They knew I loved boiled peanuts and the little town they moved to was famous for them. They would bring me peanuts every year as long as they could drive.

The McMords sold their home and they don't visit anymore. I am sure it's because they can't drive anymore. Before they moved, their son had a friend that moved back home who was looking for someone to dust, mop and vacuum. I went and he was remarkable. His name was Mr. Nelson. God kept right on blessing me.

I told Mr. Nelson how much I charged but after I worked the first day he set his own price and gave me a tip. I was talking about cutting back on work. I told him about those that had moved or passed away. I wasn't going to take on any new people because I was getting older and all my children were grown and most of my grandchildren as well. He said he didn't blame me and that he was going to sell his house and land before I quit because he could not keep up the yard and the housework. I told him if God showed me someone to work for a while I was still well enough, I would.

Mr. Nelson began to have health problems so he got my son in law to do some repair work on his house. He put it up for sale and sold it in no time. He said he was moving downtown to be close to everything. He would go on vacation but he would still pay me because he said he knew I needed the money especially after my husband passed.

After Mr. Nelson moved, he had a friend who had an aneurysm. She was still able to function; she just needed some help cleaning. I worked for her for approximately four months when she found out she had breast cancer. She then moved in with her daughter.

A new couple moved from Texas. They went to the Methodist church. Most of my employers came through my employers that went to the same church. The new couple asked one of my employers if they know of someone who can help with housework. They gave them my phone number. They called and asked if I could help. At this point I could use another day.

Lawrence took me to their house. They were Mr. and Mrs. Shell. When I first went to work for them we got along well. The 2nd week they gave me some clothes. Mr. Shell asked me if I had seen a shirt of his he couldn't find and wondered if I took it by mistake. I was devastated. I told them that I don't steal.

Mrs. Shell said, "oh, no, you are a good worker and he did not mean you stole it."

He said, "I guess I misplaced it."

I said, "all the clothes are still in the bag you gave me: I can bring them back."

Mr. Shell said, "I'm sorry. I didn't mean to offend you."

I said, "I was raised to work for my needs and ask if I need something. My bible says ask and it shall be given."

Mrs. Shell was like Virginia, God has given me a chance to make things right. Mrs. Shell was raised in a small town north of here and her mom had a black woman that did her washing, ironing and cleaning. Her mom treated the lady well but Mrs. Shell said she didn't know then what she knows now. She had a friend back home that she asked to help her find this woman's son. The friend did.

The son was a pastor of a large Baptist church. She asked me and a few others to go to his church on Sunday. The service was good and he remembered Mrs. Shell even though he was a young boy when he originally met her. She was a big giver. She was all about Jesus and we talked and prayed a lot. She even started a bible class in her home.

Mr. Shell was a retired pilot and captain out of the Navy. He had a good heart and was a giver as well. He had a sharp mind and was good at discerning people and things. We would talk every day when I worked. I would say things my grandparents and other people I worked for had said and he would tell me it needs to be in a book. I told him that other people had said the same thing.

Every week or so he would say, "are you working on that book?" He would tease me about being on the Oprah show or my book being made into a movie. He kept encouraging me to write.

Before my husband died I would need help for medicine, sometimes food, or bills. I would pray for a financial blessing knowing that God would supply my every need. It seemed like every time it would be the week and day that I went to the Shells. When I would walk in they'd say, "Guess what? You are gonna get a bigger paycheck today."

When this happened the first time, I couldn't help but cry. I thank God and them both because I had been praying for that. This continued to happen. They also donated to help me fix up my house. They were God sent.

They would take me out to eat at some nice places in town and neighboring towns. When they would take me, I'd say I've been here before, Mrs. Scottsdale brought me here in the '80's. Mrs. Mary and Mrs. Scottsdale would take me out to eat a couple times a year and now so did the Shells. The Shells were so generous. They would give me days off with pay. This relationship will go on until - then, whenever that may be.

I felt like I knew Mrs. Mary because she had come home so many different times, holidays, deaths and anniversaries. After her mom passed away, she would see if Mr. Henry needed anything. One day Mr. Henry said, "Mary, how is it you know exactly what we need?"

She said, "I have a little bird."

He said, "is that bird named Virginia?"

Mary was always there for her family. She helped them in every way she could. She came back to stay after her and her husband divorced. She stayed with the Carols and she also helped with Ms. Alex who lived in an assisted living home. I worked at the Carols two days a week, one for the Carols and one for Mrs. Mary. Mrs. Mary had one room and a dog. The household was made up of four dogs and three people. Mrs.

Mary would pay me for both days. She gave. That's just the kind person she was. Then Mrs. Mary decided to move in with her dad. So, she would have more room.

Mrs. Mary would take care of Ms. Alex and made sure she had what she needed. She took me to see Ms. Alex and sometimes would bring Ms. Alex's clothes for me to wash and press. Mrs. Mary would try to see her two or three times a week. It was a hard time for Mrs. Mary.

When Mrs. Mary got her divorce, she began looking for an area to build her house. When her house was finished she moved all her furniture in. My family helped her move. She adopted us from day one. I cleaned her house and my grandson kept the yard. She taught him how to fertilize, weed and prune. My grandson had two children and Mrs. Mary treated them like they were her grands. They called her Aunt Lilli. Christmas was awesome for the whole family. She would leave no one out. My children and grandchildren all received presents from Mrs. Mary. She believed that everyone should have more than one gift to open on Christmas.

Mrs. Mary had moved into her home and she had more time alone and she began drinking. Sometimes when it was really bad she would call me at night and I would go see her.

I knew how I could be because I had seen it before. So, I helped how I could, when I could.

I was still working for the Carols, Henrys and Scottsdale's along with Mrs. Mary. Then Mr. Scottsdale started having health problems and then a hurricane came and the whole area was without power for two weeks. Trees fell on their property and there was damage to the house. Their children came to help. Since the house was damaged the health care nurse talked to the family about Mr. Scottsdale being on hospice care at the hospital since most places were still without power.

Mr. Scottsdale died almost three weeks later. I had worked for them for 28 years. They were family. Before Mr. Scottsdale passed and my children gave me and Lawrence a wedding to renew our vows. He was able to attend and celebrate with us. Mrs. Scottsdale helped put everything together and kept it a secret from me. Thank you, Mrs. Scottsdale, for being a friend.

My work was not much now at Mrs. Scottsdale, but she kept me coming. We would go out to eat afterwards. One day she told me about a friend that was a retired teacher that needed help. Mrs. Scottsdale took me to their home and introduced me. She told them how long I had been working with her. They were the Walkers.

I would clean and Mr. Walker would cook. Mrs. Walker had cancer and it began to spread. Mr. Walker was a good man. I had to beg her to let me help to give him a break. Mrs. Walker soon passed away but before then Mr. Walker found out he had cancer as well. I continued to work for him. He lived two years after his wife's passing.

My work life was never empty. I had a full week. Back to Mondays. I worked for Mrs. Mary. Mrs. Mary was a blessing to me, her and her family. Mrs. Mary began to get busy. She started volunteering at the church for a few hours. She even became active in the home owner's association in her community. She was the president and ran it better than ever. She then got in touch with her high school classmates and they began to meet once a month.

It wasn't long before she was planning things for them to do. She would have monthly meetings at her house. I told her they liked her house because she cooks, the house is clean and I do the cleaning up. Mrs. Mary always took me places with her out to eat, shopping, even doctor's appointments so I couldn't complain.

Mrs. Mary's niece, the Carol's daughter Rose, came home from college while I was still working at the Carols. She asked me to teach her how to separate clothes for washing and how to iron. I laughed and she said, "why are you laughing?" I told her that her grandmother had asked me to teach her. It all paid off because when she was in college she got a job at a cleaners. I met her employer and she said Rose was the best shirt presser she had ever had.

I met Rose's boyfriend and he said thanks for teaching Rose how to iron because she saved him lots of money because he did not have to take his shirts to the cleaners. He was going to be a lawyer. Everyone that I met knew me as the lady that taught Rose to iron. That was another promise I had fulfilled to the Henry family.

The Henrys had gotten up in age and had begun to get sick with the flu. She was a diabetic. I noticed one day that she was not steady on her feet and I asked her if she was okay. She said she was alright. I checked her blood sugar and it was alright. She began to walk out to the car and she fainted. I called Mrs. Carol and she came over. She was a nurse before she was a teacher. Mrs. Carol took her to the hospital; she had pneumonia.

Her children were called. Mr. Henry has to go to the hospital as well. He had pneumonia as well but he got well enough to go back home. Mrs. Carol got sick also. Mrs. Mary would come out during the day and bring soup and food. Mrs. Henry returned home with hospice and her children. Mr. Henry was getting better so Mrs. Mary would take him to see her. She passed away after being home a couple of days.

He was married to his second wife for *14* years. She was good for Mr. Henry during that time. Mrs. Mary came and picked me up for the funeral. Afterward we went to Mr. Henry's house. Her children gave me a card thanking me for being there for their mom.

Then to Thursdays. On Thursdays I worked for Mrs. Scottsdale. At this point it had been two years since her husband had passed. Their house was in the middle of land and more land. We began to think that it was unsafe for her to stay all the way out there at night alone. She said the yard was beginning to be expensive to keep up. She wanted a house with a small yard. We had been looking at homes downtown. Her children wanted her to come where they were. I didn't want her to go but I didn't have any say so.

She put the house up for sale. I kept the house clean with my daughter's help. My family would help with the yard and keep the weeds out of the garden. During this time, I had a hysterectomy so one of my friends worked for her. We kept the house clean for people to come and see it. We did this for seven months then she finally got a buyer. She sold her house and land. She decided to stay here so she moved to town in a nice neighborhood with a small yard. She asked me if I would still work for her. I said yes. I had to go that far into town to work for Mrs. Mary also.

Mr. Henry began to get his strength back but he still wasn't able to drive. Mrs. Mary drove him around and cooked for him and the Carols. Mrs. Carol began to have sick spells and we thought she was having an allergy problem. Mr. Henry had to go back to the hospital for pneumonia. That left Mrs. Mary seeing after Mr. Henry. When he came home his oxygen levels would not stay up and he became weak. Home health care came out. Slowly but surely, he regained his strength. Soon he was able to walk to the mailbox.

Mr. Henry went to the doctor. He learned that the cancer this time was incurable by doctors. He was really calm and said I am here as long as God lets me. He said he wanted to die at home. He did well for a few weeks. Hospice came in. A little later Mr. McCord told me right before I got off that an ambulance was heading to Mr. Henry's home. I ran there. The paramedics were trying to bring him out. I told them to leave him there because he wanted to die at home. They asked who I was. I tried to tell them but they wouldn't listen to me.

I said, "before you move him, call his daughter." I called Mrs. Carols on the phone. I knew they knew her because she volunteered at the fire department. Then I called hospice. They apologized after talking to her. Mr. Henry passed peacefully.

This was a man I had worked for *32* years with two wives. After Mrs. Mary and Mrs. Carol got everything out of the house they wanted. They told me along with my family to clean out the house. They got a dumpster but told us we could keep anything we wanted. I asked Mrs. Mary if we could do whatever we wanted with the stuff. She said yes. I had a good yard sale that paid for me on a trip to the Bahamas.

Mrs. Carol's health began to fade. She had a successful bone marrow transplant. Mrs. Mary went with her to encourage her to eat and take her medicine. Mrs. Carol made it through and was able to attend her daughter's wedding. She then moved to be closer to her children in Georgia. I didn't get to visit her, but she would ask me to come over and over again. She would write to me and send me pictures. Two years later Mrs. Carol passed. Mrs. Mary had lost so many people but she had a real devoted son.

The Lord placed another family in my life. Their names were the Marks. Mrs. Marks could walk a little at first but she was mostly in a wheelchair. She had great determination. I believe the Lord had me there for Mr. Marks instead of Mrs. Marks. Mr. Marks a was remarkable man but he had not done any housework prior to his wife getting sick. She did everything until she couldn't. She would cook two and three meals a day, bake cakes and cut the yard. I told her she was a Proverbs wife.

Mr. Marks confided in me about the insurance, they didn't not have any nor enough in the bank for a funeral. He sold everything he had in order to give her a good funeral. He did not know he was doing it for himself. We were shocked when he died of a heart attack a few months later. Mrs. Marks was alone with him. She never got over the experience. Her sisters came in and worked with her and one of her two sons moved in with her.

The doctor ordered her to be with hospice. She didn't want them. I told her I used them with my husband and she said okay. She asked me if I would come visit her once a week. The last time I went to visit her she could barely talk but managed that she loved me and appreciated all that I had done. She passed away less than a week later.

I was still working for Mrs. Mary at the time. One of her classmates told her about a doctor they knew down south that could do surgery on her back. Mrs. Mary checked with her insurance and it was a go. She asked her son to please take off of work to go with her because she had to fly down. She's in great shape after eight weeks of healing. Mrs. Mary then really began doing things. When some of her classmates were sick she would cook meals for them. Then she became a diabetic. Mrs. Mary made me promise that I would keep working for her because she knew I would keep her house clean.

Mrs. Mary had a nervous breakdown after a fire. Mrs. Mary went to the bathroom, pulled her oxygen off and laid it on the table with a cigarette in an ashtray. She forgot to turn the oxygen off. The cigarette set the oxygen on fire but the tank did not blow up. Thank God. The drapes caught fire and the alarm went off. The neighbor heard it and went over to check. The neighbor called the fire department. That day scared Mrs. Mary. We could not get her back into that room. She would sleep in her favorite chair in the family room.

One Monday I went in and Mrs. Mary was slumped over in her chair. The caregiver was crying. I called the neighbor who was a retired nurse. The neighbor called the doctor and her son, Mitchell. Mrs. Mary went to the hospital. She came to herself and asked me not to leave her and to please be there for her son. Mitchell came home and worked from there. I kept my same work days. Then Mrs. Mary went from hospital to rehab. Mrs. Mary went back to the hospital after Mitchell went back to his home.

The doctor called and said Mrs. Mary probably won't make it through the night. We went to the hospital praying, asking her to hold on until Mitchell got there and she did. We stayed with Mitchell the whole time. It was about three weeks when they took Mrs. Mary off the respirator to see how much she could breathe on her own. Her breathing and kidneys began to improve. Then she caught pneumonia and an infection. A few days later she had to have surgery. She made it through okay.

A few days later Mrs. Mary moved from the hospital to selective specialty. Mrs. Mary was there for a few weeks before she came around. Mrs. Mary opened her eyes so they called Mitchell to let him know. She got well enough to visit home on her birthday. Then she was not doing so well, she had to go back to the hospital. I was talking to Mrs. Mary and we would say scriptures and the last thing she said to me was, "I love you." Mrs. Mary had never said those words to me. She never said it but she definitely showed it. I was shocked. Those were the last words I heard her say. Then she too passed away. At this point I was used to death and could see the beauty in it especially if it comes peacefully and you are in the Lord's hands.

Working continued. Mitchell kept me on payroll just like Mary did. Mitchell was generous and gave away so many things. I didn't count the boxes but it took me months to pack up the items. It was *40* years with the Henry family and now their grandson. I don't know how far this is going to go but I am loving it. I was blessed by Mrs. Mary and being blessed by her son.

I am still working with the Scottsdale's and the Shells, where this will conclude, only God knows. God has blessed my life tremendously from my upbringing, my family and the people I have worked for. This life has not always been full of daisies but it has always had a purpose, to help. Whether it was the little girl on the farm or the mature woman being there for friends. Life can throw so much at you but all that matters is you remember God.

If you keep a But God with you, you could never go wrong. No matter how it may seem things can always change. Time after time, he provided. He made a way when I didn't see a way. I remained faithful in my work, and he remained faithful to me. Hard work never goes unnoticed. Even when it seems insignificant. If you are a dishwasher, be the best dishwasher you can be. My life may not have been glamorous and I have had humble beginnings but this was my story and I am blessed just to be able to tell it. I did not always think this was possible, But God. With God all things are possible, regardless of its size.

# Acknowledgements

In appreciation of the guidance and wisdom provided by my Lord and Savior.

A very Special thanks to my mom, Emma Coleman, and my grandparents, Jim and Annie Bell Simpson for Everything.

Thanks to everyone that I have crossed paths with throughout my journey writing this book, your encouragement mean a lot.

This is a very thoughtful list of people that was very influential to the publishing of this book:

Lillie S.- my best friend who has been there for me and my family my entire life since school.

James S.- who kept encouraging me to continue to write.

Mary R.- who was an employer as well as a wonderful friend not only to me but to my family.

Marjorie G.- an employer, a friend that help all of this come to pass.

Larshielle B and Latana S.- for proof reading, typing and formatting.

Elizabeth C., Jackie F., John G., James M., Carolyn T., Alice H., Evelyn W., Lil K., for encouragement.

Deyon L., for leading me in the right direction to publishing.

Last but not least author Kendrick W., who put my words on paper so you could read them.

SO YOU CAN WRITE
**PUBLICATIONS**®

"Where the writers go…"

www.sycwp.com

www.ingramcontent.com/pod-product-compliance
Lightning Source LLC
Chambersburg PA
CBHW052009090426
42741CB00008B/1617